Lean MRP

Establishing a Manufacturing Pull System for Shop Floor Execution Using ERP or APS

SECOND EDITION

David Altemir

This publication is designed to provide accurate and authoritative information with regard to the subject matter covered. It is sold with the understanding that the author and publisher is not engaged in rendering legal, accounting, or other professional services. If legal advice or other expert assistance is required, the services of a competent professional person should be sought.

ISBN: 9781719918107

Table of Contents

Acknowledgements

I would like to give my personal thanks and gratitude to all of the following people who informed my writing of this book and influenced and supported me over the years:

- My wife, Beata, who has inspired me and nearly everyone she has met with her enormous warmth, heart, caregiving, and inner strength. She is the light of my life

- My mother, Anne-Marie, who taught me the power of doing, hard work, and unconditional love

- My stepfather, Bill, who accepted me as his own and endlessly supported me through thick and thin

- All my past employers, employees, co-workers, and clients who generously allowed me an opportunity to work, learn, and contribute, particularly Dr. John Langford, John Tylko, Ron Richman, Bill Anderson, and Ray Hazeldine who helped accelerate my career by entrusting me with growing management responsibilities

- Bob Labelle, Robert May, Mitch Bedinger, and Bill Anderson who worked with me vigorously to promote positive operational changes

- All my former classmates and friends throughout the years who supported me with kindness, generosity, encouragement, and good times

- The late Drs. John Margrave, Richard Smalley, and David McKay – Giants of fluorine chemistry, carbon chemistry, and lunar geology who generously led their research

Acknowledgements

teams, made world-changing contributions, and inspired my respect in the scientific method

- All the academics and practitioners of manufacturing management that have paved the road before us

About the Author

David Altemir

Contact at:

david@altemirconsulting.com

www.altemirconsulting.com

David Altemir has over 25 years of professional experience in engineering, R&D, manufacturing, supply chain management, and IT. His diverse experience has spanned spacecraft, aircraft, UAVs, helicopters, medical devices, software development, contract manufacturing, and other industries at nearly all levels and operating areas. Mr. Altemir has helped companies ranging from $3 million to $3 billion in revenue, as well as pre-revenue start-ups, to meet growing customer demand with on-time delivery and high quality. His career has been marked by instituting numerous transformational improvements.

Lean MRP is the result of his many years of work as a manufacturing manager and introduces important innovations and techniques for production scheduling and control.

Mr. Altemir holds a Bachelor of Mechanical Engineering from the University of Texas at Austin, Master of Materials

About the Author

Science from Rice University, and MBA from the Massachusetts Institute of Technology. He is also a certified Lean Six Sigma Sensei.

Mr. Altemir currently resides in Dallas, TX and is managing principal of Altemir Consulting, which is available for consulting engagements. He particularly enjoys working with small and medium size businesses eager to get to the next level. Areas of specialization include:

- On-time performance
- Production capacity, rates, and output
- Production planning, scheduling, and control
- Purchasing
- Inventory management
- Manufacturing costs and product margins
- Bill of material management
- Engineering change management
- Product quality
- New product introduction and time-to-market
- Sales forecasting
- Sales, Inventory, and Operations Planning (SIOP)
- IT system development, implementation, and optimization
- Employee training
- ISO 9001 process development
- Turnaround management
- Cash flow and business valuation improvement
- New site development

1.   Introduction

1.1. Wait a Minute … I Thought MRP was "Push", Not "Pull"

This book explains how to establish effective ERP production scheduling as a precursor to implementing a Lean manufacturing pull system on the shop floor by mimicking the behavior of traditional kanbans. Those of you already familiar with kanbans know that they provide a superior mechanism for managing material flow within a factory that minimizes material shortages, work-in-process (WIP) inventory, and manufacturing lead times. So why not just implement kanbans in the normal way throughout the factory thereby eliminating the need for production scheduling altogether? The answer in some organizations is a resounding "yes … if only it was that easy!" Even for those managers that yearn for a pull-based system, there are some manufacturing environments (such as in aerospace, industrial equipment, and contract manufacturing) where the use of kanbans and supermarkets can be challenging or even impractical. The variables are just too many and traditional *kanbans* are in some cases ill-equipped to cope with changing demand. Continuous improvements may have, in some cases, been successful in establishing isolated islands of Lean flow within the overall operation. But many may feel that these improvements were limited in their impact and only skirted the periphery of what was possible in realizing observable bottom-line results.

So how can we use MRP or APS to implement a *Lean manufacturing control system* that improves manufacturing flow, minimizes lead times, and reduces in-process inventories in environments where previous Lean initiatives fell short? How can our Lean initiatives yield transformational improvements at the corporate level rather than merely providing a smattering of isolated shop floor improvements? The answers lie in using the power of the computer to help achieve Lean flow in much the same way that traditional physical approaches do. As we will see, an automated planning or scheduling system can be a key part of meeting this challenge not by dictating when operations must start or finish but rather by providing a useful set of shop floor priorities. Focusing on the *order* in which work must proceed rather than the dates that the work must start and finish begins to introduce a control system element that will be useful in creating *pull* in complex manufacturing environments. It is only then that the prospect of producing "the right part at the right time" can more easily be achieved.

Lean MRP, as you will see, acts like a traffic control system that reduces congestion and travel time for materials and products flowing in a factory.

1.2. Who Needs Lean MRP?

This book is for those manufacturing managers who have always strived for a Lean operation but nevertheless feel that an ERP system offers a more practical and scalable solution for managing a complex and turbulent shop floor. For them, the prospect of *Lean MRP* offers an exciting opportunity to positively and comprehensively transform the whole of their operation.

The reason that some manufacturing operations continue to rely on production schedules is understandable. These environments are "pull-resistant" because they are often characterized by a high mix of products and part numbers. Figure 1 illustrates this high-mix situation, which is also known as the classic N/1 scheduling problem. This archetypical problem asks how best to schedule *N* number of part numbers all competing for a single resource, say a milling machine or any other type of manufacturing work center. *N* can be extremely large in some real-world cases. Ideally, each part number would have dedicated resources and work would proceed in a linear production line.

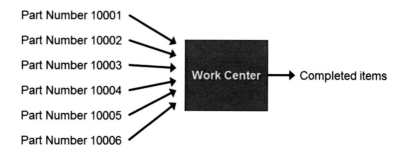

Figure 1. Classic N/1 scheduling problem.

Although linear production lines may be common in light bulb factories, other industries such as aerospace, industrial equipment, and contract manufacturing don't have the real estate or capital necessary for such efficient operation. An aircraft factory, for example, involves thousands or tens of thousands of part numbers that must magically come together as a final product. It is almost inevitable that the N/1 problem will appear very prominently in these kinds of operations. Manufacturers in these industries don't have the luxury of linear production lines. What they end up with instead is a "job shop" environment as shown in Figure 2. The job shop is indeed dominated by work centers of the "N/1" variety. The balance of supply and demand is complex and ever-changing, so much so that MRP is often seen as the only practical approach to establishing a workable control system that can be deployed widely and comprehensively.

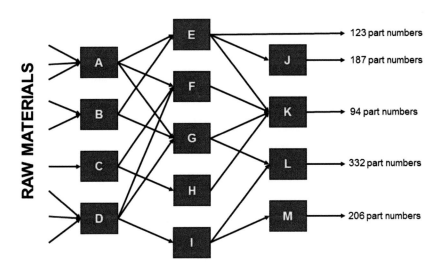

Figure 2. Simplified representation of material flow between work centers within a job shop.

Despite its practical advantages, MRP and ERP systems have often been maligned not only because they are perceived as being inconsistent with the *pull* paradigm but also because of the instability of calculated schedule dates – often referred to as system *nervousness* or *volatility*. Schedule volatility has a significant negative impact on an organization's ability to execute successfully. A schizophrenic system that cannot make up its mind as to when material quantities are needed is indeed no system at all. This situation inevitably leads to the use of overhead-intensive workarounds such as manual expediting, spreadsheets, custom reports, or stand-up daily meetings to make up for what the system is unable (or at least is perceived to be unable) to provide. These workarounds often create a death spiral in which the schedule is not believed and is therefore not followed. Because the schedule is not followed, the plan that the system generated sooner or later comes face to face with the incongruent reality of what has transpired on the shop floor (via the input of labor and inventory transactions). The system must necessarily "catch up" to all the workarounds and schedule deviations that were carried out thus driving the calculation of a new and different schedule solution during the next scheduling iteration. This is akin to entering 5 + 5 into a calculator and correctly getting a result of 10. If 5 + 5 is entered again the next day, the same result is produced. However, if the inputs are changed to say 5.1 + 4.7, then a different result is obtained, which is then perceived as system nervousness. We will be focusing on how to minimize these changing inputs and eliminate undesirable system feedback loops to stabilize system performance[1].

However, even if we do meaningfully reduce system nervousness, we are still left with the apparent limitation that MRP systems are fundamentally incapable of supporting the *pull* paradigm. Solutions often promoted by software developers and sales consultants that seek to overcome this limitation include advanced production scheduling (APS). APS systems go beyond traditional MRP by employing sophisticated scheduling techniques and pegging logic to produce an "optimal production schedule". The assertion that APS systems with their superior planning methodologies are "more responsive to dynamic production environments" and respond more readily to the "realities of the shop floor" provide intuitive and compelling selling points. References to Lean terminology and principles invariably creep into the sales presentations and implementation campaigns for these systems. Despite the allure of these technological approaches and the promises they seek to deliver, these attempts to reach manufacturing nirvana often fall short of expectations putting the goals of Lean execution seemingly even further out of reach. In fact, the ways that these systems are employed often not only result in a higher level of nervousness than their simpler MRP counterparts, they can also violate important fundamental

---

[1] Note that MRP volatility is not always caused by people "changing things". Sometimes the system is inherently volatile because of how it was set up and/or is used as we will see later.

planning and scheduling principles that prevent effective control of the production process and irreversibly destroy valuable management information. A negative byproduct of these efforts is renewed frustration among stakeholders when the promise of a new approach fails to be realized through fruitless implementation and transition pains.

1.3. What are Our Objectives?

The *Lean MRP* approach described in this book aims at four principal objectives:

- Maximize on-time completions thereby maximizing customer satisfaction

- Reduce manufacturing lead times

- Reduce work-in-process (WIP) inventory

- Enable accurate forward-looking schedule projections to support the making of reliable promises to the customer

This approach of using the computer to establish an optimized shop floor control system will enable easier implementation, improved scalability, and prospects for the dynamic control of "virtual kanbans" in response to fluctuating demand within a job shop environment. By doing so, we will be using customer demand to *pull* material at all levels in the factory dynamically. As a bonus, we will also be able to deliver schedule projections to product managers and salespeople that accurately predict when products will be completed and ready for shipment.

1.4. What is Necessary to Effectively Apply Lean Principles with MRP?

The following conditions must be met to effectively achieve Lean execution in complex manufacturing environments using MRP:

1. The fundamental ability of the company to make products with a high level of manufacturing quality must be secure as no planning or scheduling methodology can be expected to make up for such shortcomings.

2. A baseline operating plan must be developed that meets customer demand and is respected by its stakeholders because it is stable, realistically executable, and provides a benchmark against which to measure performance and generate management information.

3. Customer demand cannot be allowed to vacillate unrestrained based on the last customer who complained or because a certain product manager demands it. Natural fluctuations in the market are one thing, but repeated and habitual revisions of customer due dates are quite another. Manufacturing is often a big ship that cannot easily be turned. Objective rules of engagement are therefore needed to govern when customer due dates (and therefore shop floor priorities) may be changed.

4. The baseline plan needs to be conveyed to the shop floor in a way that provides *customer-driven* work priorities for every operation, material, component, and assembly. It must also objectively and fairly expose what work is late, early, and on-time.

5. We need a way to provide visual signals to shop floor personnel that effectively communicate customer demand and employ a *regulatory mechanism* to mediate Lean flow.

6. Frequent schedule projections should be made to identify schedule risks so resources can be reallocated as necessary. This will be the company's "early warning system". It will also provide accurate estimated completion dates (ECDs) suitable for making reliable promises to the customer.

These are the tactical objectives we will be pursuing in the coming chapters.

With a high level of manufacturing quality assumed to be in place, we will see how to establish a planning and scheduling system that provides a stable set of work priorities and schedule targets to drive the supply chain. These form the Lean *Baseline Schedule* – a schedule that, as we will see, will be differentiated from a traditional MRP "push" schedule more as a result of how we choose to interpret it and adhere to it than the way in which it has been created. A happy consequence of this approach is that most any ERP-based planning system will suffice. In many cases, no additional investment is required. However, a well-crafted plan by itself is necessary but insufficient to establish Lean flow. The plan must also have an effective interface with the factory that provides the regulatory mechanism needed to truly drive Lean *execution*. As we will also see, incorporating a regulatory mechanism into the shop floor operation is the secret to driving Lean flow in a complex environment using ERP, MRP, or APS.

Any schedule is, at best, only a theoretical blueprint for the planned outcomes we desire. It does nothing to ensure that they will actually come to fruition. There will be instances when we will deviate from the plan. How we choose to manage these deviations is what will determine the operating performance of the business. It determines whether inventory will be allowed to pile up before it is really needed or if shortages will be allowed. It determines what the overhead cost of support functions such as scheduling, expediting, or dispatching will be in order to execute workarounds or develop schedule recovery plans. It can also be a primary determinant in how nervous our planning system is.

I hope that this introduction has stimulated your interest in cooking now ways to maximize operational performance. This is not the usual "yada-yada". The concept of *Lean MRP* is a novel one, which holds the promise of comprehensive, positive, and transformational change.

Chapter 1 – Introduction

2.   Essential Concepts

2.1. What is the Fundamental Difference Between "Push" and "Pull"?

"Push" and "pull" are terms that refer to the two different mechanisms used to control when material (and therefore work) is transferred from one work center to the next. A way to determine whether the "push" or "pull" principle is at play is to ask yourself what *exactly* is providing the impetus for material moving from one place to another within the factory? This facet of a manufacturing control system is sometimes referred to as "flow control" or "in/out control". Note that I use the term "material" in a very general sense as it may refer to raw material, components, assemblies, or products at any point in the manufacturing process.

To put it simply, a push system causes material to move forward in the manufacturing process based on forecasted time estimates regardless of whether the next work center is ready to work on it or not. This approach can lead to material piling up in front of work centers, thus leading to higher than necessary work-in-process (WIP) inventory levels and longer lead times.

In contrast, material moves forward in a pull system only when the next work center needs the material to satisfy customer demand and is ready to accept it. It is therefore easy to see why a pull paradigm is more desirable for minimizing WIP inventory and manufacturing lead times.

However, minimizing WIP inventory and lead times are not enough. We are additionally obligated to maintain a production rate that meets customer demand. For that, we can use the Theory of Constraints to identify and resolve bottlenecks so that adequate production rates can be achieved. The Theory of Constraints together with the principles of Lean Manufacturing are therefore both essential to effectively solving a variety of fundamental manufacturing problems. I say this to point out that the use of a "pull system" may not be a panacea to cure all ills as it must also be accompanied by high in-process quality (i.e., low defect rate) and sufficient throughput (i.e., production rate) capability.

2.2. How is a Work Center like a Kanban?

Let's take a detailed look at the pull paradigm by deconstructing the operating principles of a kanban so that we will later be able to understand how we can replicate these fundamental ideas in the context of an MRP-driven operation. The ultimate goal is to devise "virtual kanbans" based on MRP data that can be used to achieve Lean flow.

The first thing we notice is that the maximum amount of material that a kanban can hold is a predetermined level known as the *kanban quantity*. This quantity can be calculated in many different ways, but it suffices to say that it must be an amount sufficient to supply the downstream work center with a minimal risk of material shortages. A simple yet effective way to calculate the kanban quantity is:

$$kanban\ quantity\ =\ \mu L + N\sqrt{L}\sigma$$

where μ is the average demand imposed by the downstream work center for a given material item typically measured in units per day, L is the average lead time for producing that material item, N is a safety factor (often between 1.2 and 4.0), and σ is the standard deviation of demand. Note that the second term on the right-hand side of the equation addresses the variability in demand. The inclusion of this term is essential and cannot be ignored since spikes in demand can and do cause materials to be quickly consumed thus leading to shortages.

Most of us are familiar with kanbans consisting of two or more bins. If, for example, we had a five-bin Kanban, we would simply take the kanban quantity as calculated above and divide it by five to determine how much material is needed for each bin.

However, let's consider for the moment the hypothetical case of a one-bin kanban. This is useful because, as we will see in a moment, we will model each work center in the factory as a one-bin kanban. In the one-bin case, material will be allowed to enter whenever material falls below the kanban quantity just as it did for the multi-bin case. One approach we can take is to make the input quantity of material entering the kanban variable. For example, if the kanban is short 25 units, we would add 25 units; if it is short two units, we would introduce two units; and so on. We are not bound to integral multiples of the individual bin quantities as we were for the multiple-bin case.

We now have a definition for the *input condition* for a one-bin kanban. The quantity of material that we can introduce without violating the kanban quantity is:

$$input\ quantity = kanban\ quantity - current\ actual\ quantity$$

What about the *exit condition*? What is the impetus for material exiting the kanban? Well, if we are modeling each work center as a kanban, we can then imagine a string of kanbans each one feeding the next to represent a manufacturing process as shown in Figure 3. In this case, completed work would move forward whenever the next work center's input condition is met.

Figure 3. Four sequential work centers in a manufacturing process modeled as four kanbans feeding each other.

There is no theoretical conflict between the function of a one-bin kanban versus a multi-bin kanban. In both cases, the factory is working to replenish the kanban so that the kanban quantity is maintained. Material shortages will be avoided as long as we do this and the kanban quantity remains valid. However, from a practical point of view, we recognize that there is a benefit to having multiple bins since empty bins serve as convenient and easily understandable visual signals that will trigger employees to refill them. Don't feel bad that our one-bin approach does away with visual signals. It does not. In general, we are allowed any kind of visual signal to communicate that the input condition has been triggered. It can be an empty bin, a kanban card, or colored light. Even a fog horn could be used to signal that material is needed by the next work center in our pull system. For our purposes, however, we will use an electronic Dispatch List screen at each work center driven by shop floor data to signal what work needs to be done and when it can be moved forward. The mechanical details of the Dispatch List will be discussed in Chapter 6. For now, it's enough to know that the Dispatch List is the critical element that uses MRP and ERP information to enable the pull paradigm on the shop floor.

To review, we mathematically summarize below how a one-bin kanban functions and, in so doing, we have the theoretical underpinnings that will allow us to use MRP data to drive Lean material flow based on the pull paradigm. For a given work center n:

Kanban Quantity (K): $\quad K_n = \mu_n L_n + N\sqrt{L_n}\sigma_n$

Input Condition: $\quad Q_{actual,n} < K_n$

Input Quantity (Q_{in}): $\quad Q_{in,n} = K_n - Q_{actual,n}$

Exit Condition: $\quad Q_{actual,n+1} < K_{n+1}$

Exit Quantity (Q_{out}): $\quad Q_{out,n} = K_{n+1} - Q_{actual,n+1}$

We will come back to this later when we set up our Dispatch Lists to provide Lean executional signals to the shop floor.

There is one more issue to address relative to our one-bin kanban model. Normally, when we employ kanbans in a real-world shop floor setting, each bin is dedicated to supporting a single part number. After all, it wouldn't make sense to lump ten different part numbers into a single kanban. So how then, if we are using one-bin kanbans to represent work centers, do we wrestle with the fact that each work center must be able to accommodate multiple part numbers as we discussed originally in Chapter 1? Our mathematical description of a one-bin kanban tacitly assumes an average and standard deviation of demand for a single part number. To that concern, I say don't worry. We will end up generalizing and applying our one-bin model in a way that allows every work center in the factory to optimally accommodate any number of part numbers using Lean principles. This makes our solution scalable so it can support virtually any job shop regardless of its size or complexity. Please stay tuned.

2.3. What is a Production Schedule For?

A clear understanding of what is the fundamental purpose of a production schedule is something that is often taken for granted. What information do we expect to get out of a schedule? Do we want to know what work is late? Do we want to know when work is expected to be completed? Most of us will answer yes to these last two questions as they both represent valid management concerns. However, it is important to know that the underlying assumptions needed to calculate schedules that achieve both of these aims are completely different and mutually exclusive! If a company takes a one-sided approach to production scheduling, it will then be very likely that production scheduling will eventually be seen as "lacking something" that prevents it from effectively supporting manufacturing operations. This chapter should help provide some clarity and direction for those managers that find themselves in this situation.

In researching this book, I looked at published works that addressed the subject of production scheduling going as far back as the 1940s. These prior works put a special emphasis on how to construct a one-dimensional schedule whose central aim is to estimate when work will be completed. By "one-dimensional", I mean that the schedule is a linear string of points in time (i.e., dates and/or times) as shown in Figure 4 that all describe when activities are likely to start and finish based on certain assumptions.

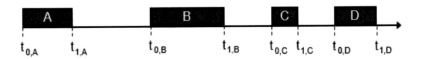

Figure 4. Four sequential activities each with estimated start and finish times.

I want to submit to you the idea that a one-dimensional production schedule cannot meet all of a manufacturing organization's business objectives. The reason for this has a lot to do with our interest in knowing what the general schedule health of our factory is. We want to know whether a particular job is late or on-time. Maybe it's on-time now but it may become late at some further point in the process because of what has transpired with other jobs. Let's understand that it is important to be able to answer these questions not just for a job overall but for all the operations that comprise each job along the way. We would be practicing poor risk management if we only focused on the estimated completion dates (ECDs) of the job and left it to the operators or supervisors to figure out the rest. Doing this would be a recipe for ugly surprises cropping up after it's too late to resolve them.

Let's be clear that there is one way, and only one way, to know whether a manufacturing operation is late: We know an operation is late when the operation is actually completed (or projected to be completed) *after* our conception of when we think it *should* have been completed. In other words, if operation X was completed on Thursday and it was planned for a Monday completion, then it's late. We can take the same approach for determining which operations have been started on-time or late. We begin to see that a second dimension to our schedule is needed in order to form our conception of "late" and "on-time" work.

Distilling this idea further, we can say that any operating parameter can be assessed to be either in "good" or "bad" health whenever its actual value (or projected value) is compared to a baseline so it can be judged against some criteria. I would therefore like to propose the following schedule health criteria that can be used universally throughout the manufacturing supply chain, both for manufactured or purchased items:

Late: $t_{actual} > T_{baseline}$

Projected to be late: $t_{projected} > T_{baseline}$

On-Time: $t_{actual} \leq T_{baseline}$

Projected to be on-time $t_{projected} \leq T_{baseline}$

where *t* can either be a start or finish time for an internal manufacturing or external supplier resource and *T* is a due date. In the case of an end-item product, the due date would typically be customer-imposed via the customer's Purchase Order. For non-deliverable parts and sub-assemblies, due dates for each part number would be internally imposed as part of what we will call a *Baseline Schedule*. The *Baseline Schedule* will be distinguished from a *Projected Schedule*, which is a different type of schedule that will be updated dynamically to estimate when future work will be completed.

To dispel any ideas that it is acceptable to drive the factory with a Projected Schedule, let's acknowledge that the Projected

Schedule moves sympathetically with the progress attained by the shop floor or supplier. If they face challenges that lead to delay, projected dates will move to the right. Conversely, if they make progress sooner than expected, projected dates will move to the left. The way in which scheduled dates move based on what has actually transpired can be problematic. It can lead to a "tail-wagging-the-dog" situation if a dynamic schedule is used to guide work on the shop floor. This is what is referred to as a feedback loop in control system theory. To put it in a manufacturing context, it is therefore useful to point out that:

> **The purpose of a production schedule is to drive the shop floor. Not vice versa.**

If we accept this assertion, then we can conclude that a Baseline Schedule that is stable and primarily reflective of customer demand is the best way to convey priorities and drive manufacturing activities. To do otherwise would allow dangerous feedback loops to arise that can induce volatility and produce an ever-changing set of targets for the organization to meet. Worst yet, when a Projected Schedule is running the shop floor, are the endless calories and dollars expended by teams of "production schedulers" or "expeditors" actively "managing" the schedule or developing shop floor workarounds without clear rules of engagement. The job titles of individuals involved in this form of active management tend to include terms such as "production scheduler" or "expeditor". However, I have a more descriptive term for this type of organizational role: "schedule destroyer". Employees that work in organizations that practice this approach tend to suffer from high blood pressure, anxiety, feelings of helplessness, and general bad feelings. There is a feeling of running as hard as you can but not getting anywhere. These types of approaches are not helpful and may suggest that there is something sorely lacking in the areas of demand planning, production scheduling, production control, manufacturing, quality, or all of these.

The use of a stable baseline tends to be practiced at firms that only utilize standard MRP since it has the best prospects for delivering a stable schedule. However, once firms choose to employ APS to "improve" their production scheduling, they feel compelled to take advantage of all of the sophisticated "active", "dynamic", and "optimized" scheduling functionality that these systems offer. The practice of running the shop floor using a production schedule that dynamically responds to changing real-world conditions is so widespread that we should take a look at it in terms of control system theory to justify what I am promoting here as an alternative approach.

2.4. Different Schedules for Different Aims

At this point, I think we're ready to clearly define four different types of schedules that we can recognize as playing useful roles in enabling Lean shop floor control and generating valuable management information. Let's outline them now:

Baseline Schedule (B): Defines due dates when an activity _should_ happen consistent with customers' expectations

Projected Schedule (P): Estimates when future activities _will_ happen consistent with all the realities of the shop floor and suppliers and the progress that has been accomplished to date

Completed Schedule (Cmp): Records when activities actually _did_ happen as a matter of historical record

Capacity Schedule (Cap): Enables manufacturing load and capacity reporting useful for

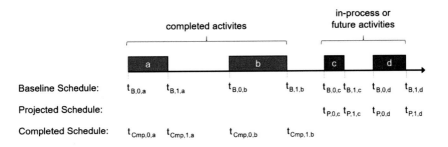

Figure 5. Anatomy of a 3D schedule.

That means that we really need a way to track daily activities in the three dimensions depicted in Figure 5.   This is what we can now refer to as a "3D production schedule". Note that the Capacity schedule has been excluded from this context because it is used for periodic management reviews rather than as a daily shop floor management tool.

Figure 6 offers an alternate way of visualizing a 3D schedule, this time as a function of progress. This visualization shows us an activity (you can regard it as either a single job, multiple jobs, or any other subset of manufacturing order fulfillment) that increasingly attains a level of progress over time. In this example, we can see that this activity is behind schedule (i.e., late) both currently in a de facto sense (since the 40% progress mark was in fact reached much later than what was stipulated in the Baseline) as well as projected to be late in the future.

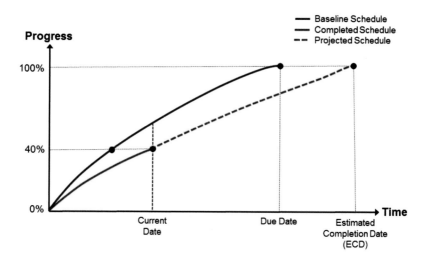

Figure 6. Trajectory representation showing Baseline, Actual, and Projection (i.e., a "3D schedule").

The Baseline and Projected Schedules each have important characteristics that must be maintained. First of all, the Baseline Schedule must be stable. It must be allowed to change only when the customer's expectations changes. It must remain immune to any supply-side influences. That means that the Baseline Schedule must be held constant despite employees reporting sick, machines breaking down, or Manufacturing or any external supplier falling behind. The Baseline is simply the idealized "voice of the customer" percolated down through all levels of the bills of materials, which changes only when the customers' requirements change.

The Projected Schedule, in contrast, is dynamic. It responds to changes in available manufacturing capacity, the myriad quality and engineering change-induced delays, as well as when suppliers report late deliveries. You might say that the

Projected Schedule is immersed in the "real world" of the manufacturer and, as a result, should be updated at least daily.

Labels such as "ECD" and "due date" should be familiar to you. A due date may be imposed either internally by management or externally by a customer. But let me reinforce that the internally imposed due date for a distinct manufacturing operation at any point in the manufacturing process must primarily flow from the customer-imposed end-item due date. This is the "secret sauce" that ensures that the whole of the Baseline Schedule, which will be used to drive manufacturing execution, will be maximally conducive to satisfying customer demand. Managing these due dates is a discipline that will be addressed in Chapter 6.

So let's return to the titular subject of the last section: What is the purpose of a production schedule? Well, we now see that the "schedule" really has three elements necessary to comprehensively address all matters of daily shop floor schedule health for the business. Table 1 summarizes what I consider to be the purposes of these three schedule elements.

Table 1. Business purposes for each of the four production schedules.

Schedule Element:	Purpose:
Baseline	Provides customer-driven schedule priorities for executing work on the shop floor and external supply chain
Projected	Provides a forward-looking forecast useful for management and customer-facing employees (e.g., sales people, product managers, executives) to manage expectations
Completed	Provides a historical date record of past activities useful for developing metrics of past performance
Capacity	Provides management with a view of load versus capacity useful for guiding capital and human resource planning

Here's the problem: The scheduling assumptions and system options needed to generate each of these schedules are *completely different.* The problem doesn't really lie with the Completed schedule. Everyone accepts that actual starts and finishes can and will be recorded. It's the Baseline and Projected Schedule that we really need to focus on. Every MRP, ERP, or APS system I am aware of cannot manage Baseline and Projected Schedules simultaneously at all levels of the bill of materials without either modification or special effort. Sadly, consultants and software developers rarely ever address or acknowledge this and hence the low level of satisfaction inherent with ERP production scheduling in the field. As you read on, I will suggest ways to achieve this level of in a practical, manageable, and effective way.

Some of you will be familiar with the concepts of Baselines and Projections as a well-accepted paradigm for project management. I am just applying the same principles to manufacturing and supply chain management that a project manager would normally use to manage a project. Microsoft Project has been doing this for years. Really nothing too special here as far as schedule management is concerned except that manufacturing-centric production scheduling software doesn't tend to support it and, as a consequence, it is rarely practiced. As you continue to read I hope we can work together to change that.

2.5. *Customer Orders: The Locomotives Pulling the Train*

As was demonstrated earlier, every activity needs to have Baseline, Projected, and Completed Schedule dates so that its schedule health can fully be known. The shipping of finished product certainly is an activity that falls within these guidelines. Customer Orders (also referred to as Sales Orders) play a special role in the manufacturing process in that they act as the true voice of the customer from which the Baseline Schedule flows as illustrated in Figure 7.

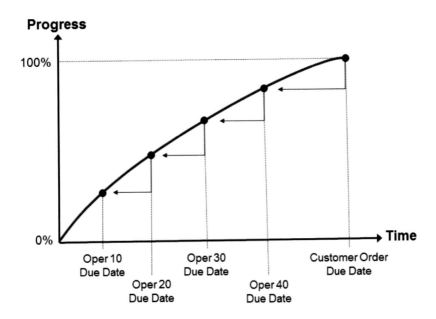

Figure 7. Baseline Schedule for a single end-item involving four manufacturing operations.

When discussing Customer Order dates, we must be careful with terminology because different systems refer to dates differently. There can be dates called "Due Dates", "Promise Dates", "MRP Dates", "Need Dates", or "Request Dates" which can mean very different things in different systems. It is important to really understand how your system treats each of these dates in order to successfully navigate this mine field. It is also critically important for all the individuals charged with Customer Order entry to have the correct understanding of what each date field is for. I will attempt to use generically descriptive terms when discussing dates to get my points across.

First, each Customer Order line item must contain a field that defines the *customer's due date*. This is usually the date that they are requesting delivery of the product at their dock. Second, each Customer Order line item must also contain a field that defines the factory's *internal due date*. The time span between these two dates is the planned shipping transit time as shown in Figure 8. This shouldn't be a problem because most systems tend to have these fields. The internal due date is just the date that MRP uses as a starting point by which generate its MRP schedule.

Additionally, it would be nice if each Customer Order line item had a third date field to contain the projected completion date (i.e., "ECD", or in some systems, the "Promise Date"). My preference is to customize an automated writeback to an existing Customer Order line item field in the database so that the APS module can have a place to publish it. I do this because customer-facing people tend to have access to the Customer Orders and it is convenient and useful to have the baseline due dates and projected ECDs both in the same place whenever they are responding to customers or product managers inquiring about specific orders.

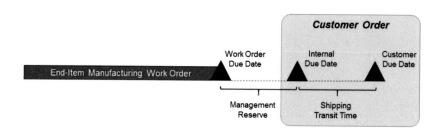

Figure 8. Baseline Customer Order dates.

We now know that we need both a Baseline Schedule that consists of stable due dates at all levels of the bill of materials and a Projected Schedule whose aim is to predict final outcomes and is dynamically updated. Chapter 5 will provide some guidance on how to manage customer baseline due dates in a way that promotes stability in the Baseline Schedule.

Chapter 2 – Essential Concepts

3.   Setting Up the System

3.1. Baseline Schedule: A Stable Operating Plan

The main feature of the Baseline Schedule is that it must express customer demand on the factory floor for all materials, operations, and jobs at all levels of the bills of materials. This means that it must be calculated using a "backwards pass" that starts with all the Customer Order line item internal due dates and then calculates lower-level dates going from right to left on the timeline. This will create a set of lower level Production Order due dates that serve as mileposts for Manufacturing to meet on the way to final completion. Most of you will recognize this as basic MRP logic.

There may be a strong compulsion to manually move Production Orders forward if there is available capacity and an opportunity to perform the work early. Please do your best to resist this temptation. That is because our Baseline Schedule must be purely an expression of customer demand rather than a statement of when the factory thinks it can best supply it. The Baseline Schedule must be maintained purely as a demand-side entity. Matters of open capacity or shop loading are supply-side issues. We shall not allow the Baseline to be affected by such considerations so that the Baseline Schedule will be effective for pulling work through the supply chain using customer demand as its motive force. Although we're concentrating here on the details of MRP and APS scheduling, let's not lose sight that the title of this book is Lean MRP and that our ultimate goals are quite lofty. These objectives require us to go beyond a conventional production scheduling approach. Our immediate goal is to establish an achievable set of "as-late-as-possible" Production Order due dates that will serve as good benchmarks against which to judge what is truly late and truly on-time from the standpoint of our external customers.

This might be a good time to address the use of graphical scheduling screens that allow production schedulers to manually drag and drop operations along the timeline. I'm strongly opposed to manual manipulation of the schedule except perhaps for some very special (and hopefully rare) situations. I generally don't allow it. I much prefer to allow scheduled operations to move under the natural influence of systematic forces configured within our automated scheduling system. The manual dragging of scheduled operations suggests the possibility that our system is not setup correctly or, worse yet, production schedulers are injecting supply-side considerations into the Baseline Schedule. Let me repeat this assertion using the red-letters-in-a-box treatment to underscore my strong words of caution against drag-and-drop schedule management:

> *Drag-and-drop scheduling is to be avoided.*
> *The perceived need to move operations around is very*
> *likely be counterproductive to establishing Lean flow.*

For those of you with APS, there's the question of whether to employ finite or infinite capacity during the backwards pass. It would be ideal for every new Customer Order that is entered to be exploded in the system using finite capacity assumptions so that it can be evaluated in the context of current shop loading and capacity conditions. This ensures that Baseline due dates can be feasibly and realistically met. However, if all the pre-existing orders in the system are also subjected to a new iteration of finite capacity calculation whenever a new order is entered, their baseline dates will very likely change. This inadvertent and frequent re-baselining should not be allowed. To guard against this source of schedule volatility, orders should be changed from "planned" to "firmed" status after suitable baseline dates have been initially determined. That means that new "planned" orders will bo introducod to the system, free to move within a sea of already "firmed" (i.e., baselined) orders using a fair and objoctivo "first come, first serve" prioritization. The scheduling engine will therefore only act on the new "planned" orders. Once firmed as part of the Baseline Schedule, these orders' place on the timeline and those customers' priority in the factory will be held fixed.

A potential pitfall is that a new Customer Order may be entered for which the resulting backwards schedule flows into the past. That is, we obtain a schedule result that says, for example, we should have started this new order last week! This is clearly an example of an infeasible customer due date which renders the resulting Baseline Schedule unrealistic and invalid. A demand planning discipline (outlined in Section 5.1) must therefore be in place to prevent the acceptance of infeasible Customer Orders so that Manufacturing can be provided with a Baseline Schedule that is realistically achievable.

Some APS systems have a very handy option to automatically switch from a backwards pass to a forward pass whenever the backwards pass fails (i.e., it crosses the current date boundary). This eliminates the need to manually iterate on the Baseline Schedule and readily offers a "best-we-can-do" due date that can be proposed back to the customer.

There are a variety of other APS system settings to be concerned about with regard to the generation of a Baseline Schedule. Frozen planning zones, for example, really shouldn't be necessary although they're not harmful if kept short, say a week or less. These kinds of settings are intended to minimize volatility, but we have already taken significant steps to maintain stability, so a frozen zone shouldn't be necessary at all. Personally, I don't use them since I want to allow orders to move freely in response to changing customer demand whenever necessary.

If you don't have APS and are relying solely on MRP, then the accuracy of your initial baselining will strongly depend on the validity of your planning lead times. On the other hand, if you do have APS, the detailed scheduling parameters defined in the routings such as run time, setup time, etc. will drive how Production Order due dates are calculated.

A special situation arises when scrap is generated and must be replaced. How then do you introduce the scrap replacement Production Order into the Baseline Schedule? My recommendation is to introduce the new Production Order using the same desired due date as the original Production Order. We should do this because customer demand, and therefore the Production Order's priority, has not changed despite the occurrence of scrap. As a consequence, the scrap replacement Production Order may very likely be late as soon as it is reaches the floor. That's OK. After all, poor quality does in fact cause production jobs to be late. We should want the scrap replacement to take on a heightened priority to hopefully catch up with the rest of the Customer Order.

The key ideas are that the Baseline Schedule must be realistically achievable, stable, and customer demand-centric. It must offer a schedule of date *priorities* that, if adhered to, will lead to on-time performance and customer satisfaction. Note that it is the priorities that the Production Order due dates convey that are really important, more so than the date values themselves. The road to improving the on-time performance of the factory begins with every operator making judicious choices as to what to work on first, then second, and so on.

Here is a summary of the general process we need to follow so we can meaningfully improve on-time performance:

1. Implement a stable and realistically achievable Baseline Schedule by properly setting up and configuring the system, allowing backwards-calculated dates to fall on the timeline under the influence of customer demand and available capacity, and practicing a good Demand Planning paradigm to minimize change activity.

2. Implement a Lean-enabled Dispatch List at each work center to convey work priorities and mediate the movement of work and materials throughout the factory.

3. Enforce adherence to the work priorities prescribed by the Baseline Schedule and communicated via the Dispatch Lists. Do this for all operators at every work center as this will be the common thread connecting and aligning all manufacturing activities to maximize a "right part at the right

time" mindset that is self-fulfilling. Develop a "priority adherence" metric and use it to manage the operation as priority adherence is a necessary prerequisite for on-time performance.

4. Measure on-time performance relative to the Baseline due dates. Develop a metric that does this for each and every work center. If priorities are being adhered to, you should see on-time performance improve accordingly.

5. Troubleshoot work centers that have poor on-time performance. Improve labor efficiency and maximize in-process quality as needed. Expand capacity at bottleneck work centers until they are de-bottlenecked and on-time performance improves.

3.2. *Completed Schedule: A Historical Record of Past Work*

Virtually every shop floor system includes labor data collection functionality that allows operators to log in and out of manufacturing operations marking the times that operations were actually started and finished. This functionality is pretty standard and setting it up is usually straightforward. What I'll focus on here are the considerations affecting the value of the data collected and the benefits it can bring.

A logical place to start is to ask how far and wide is labor data being collected in the first place? Some managers may feel that the transactional overhead associated with doing shop floor data collection just isn't worth it and adversely impacts productivity. There may be some truth to that under some circumstances. I would ask these managers to recognize that a labor collection transaction should conservatively consume only a total of 60 seconds, including both the start and finish transactions. There may be a problem if it takes longer than this. If a single operation typically takes 30 minutes to complete, then that means that these overhead transactions are occupying about 3% of employees' working time. Is that too much? Is that acceptable? It's debatable. If you picked up this book because you feel that you need a better shop floor control system, then you might conclude that paying 3% of your labor costs in favor of better shop floor control, on-time performance, order fulfillment, and customer satisfaction is a pretty good deal.

If you're still on the fence, I can suggest a shortcut to take if you're willing to sacrifice knowing actual labor costs and the ability to measure manufacturing efficiency. In this case, you can economize by eliminating "unnecessary" labor transactions and keeping only those that mark operation starts and finishes as shown in Figure 9. The net benefit of doing this is for you to weigh.

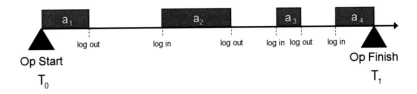

Figure 9. Manufacturing operation, *a*, completed over four separate work sessions.

What's absolutely critical is for operation finishes to be transacted correctly in a timely way when they are completed. The system must know exactly and precisely what work has been completed and what still remains to be done. This cannot be flubbed! If a job has been completed and it has been moved to the next work center but it has not been correctly transacted in the computer, then the Dispatch List screen will erroneously show work that is in fact in another work center. This is what I call "operations left open". The computer thinks the work is in one place when in fact it is physically in another. This is a problem that wreaks havoc on scheduling as well as affecting the Lean pull signals we will be setting up later. We have an entire chapter later in this book that addresses transactional discipline and provides some practical policing techniques for ensuring that employees are transacting correctly.

3.3. *Projected Schedule: The Predictor of Future Outcomes*

With the Baseline Schedule in place, we have achieved an important control system element for guiding manufacturing execution. The Projected Schedule, on the other hand, is different. It gives us the ability to gain important management information about the manufacturing operation. It serves as an informational tool rather than as an executional aid. The Baseline Schedule tells us what the *latest possible* dates are that we must meet without violating the customer's expectations flowed down to all levels. In contrast, the Projected Schedule tells us the *earliest possible* dates that can be achieved in the light of where jobs currently are in the manufacturing process and how heavily loaded the factory is.

The first requirement for implementing a Projected Schedule is that there must be a way to manage a second parallel schedule in the system that is privy to the same shop floor, material, and Customer Order inputs as the Baseline Schedule. If there are currently 8043 active Production Orders on the shop floor, then the Baseline and Projected Schedules must both contain these same 8043 Production Orders. The ability to simultaneously manage two different schedules goes beyond standard MRP. For this, your system must employ some kind of advanced scheduling capability such as APS. These systems typically provide the ability to have multiple what-if scenarios so that different assumptions can be applied. The Projected Schedule may simply be managed as a separate "what-if" scenario. These systems also often refer to the process of "scheduling" as "optimization" because they employ a variety of optimization rules that govern how dates are calculated.

Assuming that this system capability exists, we can now construct the Projected Schedule. The main assumption that must be employed is the use of a forward scheduling methodology that calculates dates, this time, moving from left to right on the timeline. No activities may be scheduled in the past. Most systems have access to the system clock and know what the current date is so they can automatically move unfinished work forward as time passes. Remarkably, some systems require a user to manually advance the clock in the scheduling program. If this is the case, this must be done each day. Either way, you must ensure that a "no-dates-in-the-past" constraint is enforced.

As mentioned before, the use of frozen scheduling horizons ("frozen fences"), in general, is not desirable as we don't want to artificially damp out legitimate date changes. This is a situation where we should be comfortable with a certain degree of dynamism provided that we have selected the appropriate scheduling assumptions. However, it is still possible for the Projected Schedule to be *too* dynamic. The best guidance I can offer here is that the scheduling assumptions used by the system must mirror the real-world practices used on the floor and those practices must themselves be stable. This statement alludes to a singular commandment that I believe should generally govern everything that individuals do when they interact with the system:

The Golden Rule:

The virtual reality of the system must match the physical reality of the shop floor and extended supply chain.

This "Golden Rule" is of paramount importance. It means that if the system says there are 1300 units of material X in inventory, then you should be able to walk over to the warehouse shelves and actually find 1300 units of that material. If a manufacturing routing says that operation 110 will be performed in work center X, then work center X must actually receive that Production Order and not pass it over to some other area of the factory without making the appropriate changes in the system to re-route the work. As was said before, the timeliness and accuracy of labor transactions are critically important in keeping the system informed of what's going on so that calculated dates, job statuses, and all sorts of other system data can be viewed with credibility and reliability as elements of the company's production control system.

If any employee sees that the system contains an error, it is incumbent upon them to correct it or, if it is a commonly encountered error, raise it to the attention of management. The procedural or system issues that allowed the error to exist must be dealt with and corrected without delay. The repeated and constant scrubbing of incorrect data, ignoring their root causes, and pursuing out-of-system workarounds "to get things done" are approaches that are sure to mitigate the usefulness of the system and undercut the organization's efforts to work more efficiently. There can be no complacency with bad data in the system. That's why there is a chapter in this book devoted to enforcing transactional discipline. The Golden Rule must be followed at all levels for all transactions, data entries, and system settings.

We now return to our original focus, the Projected Schedule, understanding that all these data management considerations affect the quality and predictive accuracy of the Projected Schedule. The practices on the shop floor, for example, to move an active job from one work center to another during the manufacturing process can significantly affect the Projected Schedule. These shop floor practices must be carefully studied and understood so that the Projected Schedule can be calculated to accurately predict future outcomes. Was there a technical feasibility reason for moving the job? If so, maybe the routing should be changed to route the work to a more appropriate work center. Maybe the work center definitions are questionable. Perhaps the job moved because the work center was overloaded. These are just a few of the myriad of issues that must be investigated to support good production scheduling. To this day, the Work Center Audit (to be discussed in Section 6.4) is the best way I know to uncover all these gremlins and weed them out.

Another scheduling consideration that is sometimes missing from out-of-the-box systems is correctly accounting for supplier performance. We have already made the case for having two separate schedules – *Baseline* and *Projected*. We now need to take a look at Purchase Orders using this same framework. That means that each deliverable line item in the Purchase Order should have two dates: One that informs the Baseline Schedule and another that informs the Projected Schedule.

Most all systems address the former consideration. The Purchase Order line items have dates called something like "Due Date", "Delivery Date", or "Dock Date" that convey when the supplier needs to make each ordered material available to us, the purchaser. I favor the term "due date" because I think it is more straightforward in characterizing the date as one that we are imposing as a requirement upon the supplier. These are the dates that suppliers take from our Purchase Orders and enter into their own systems to express the demand we are imposing on them. As should now be clear, these dates fall very well within the role of the Baseline Schedule.

The second Purchase Order date, however, is where we may encounter challenges. There really needs to be another date that can be used to capture when the supplier believes he can realistically deliver the material. Let's call this date the "projected delivery" date.

At first, the baseline due date and projected delivery dates will be the same. The projected delivery date is confirming the supplier's initial estimate that they can actually deliver it on the due date. This is trivial at this initial stage but the projected delivery date may significantly deviate from the baseline due date as time marches on.

Let's say at some later time that the supplier encounters difficulties and says that he expects a two-week delay in the delivery of one of our needed materials. If the due date is

7/1/2018, we must then update the projected delivery date and change it to 7/15/2018 as soon as we receive this bad news. We don't change the due date because our original requirement has not changed. It is also important to keep this date intact to serve as an objective benchmark for supplier performance measurement purposes later on. Our updated projected delivery date, however, becomes extremely useful in influencing the Projected Schedule so that realistic expectations can be brought to bear in developing more accurate manufacturing schedule projections.

As I said, the implementation of a projected delivery date within the Purchase Order in some systems may be missing. This is an area where some customization may be required to more effectively tie Purchase Orders to the scheduling engine to more accurately calculate manufacturing outcomes. If the system does not do this out-of-the-box, then hopefully this customization will simply consist of redefining and repurposing the date fields in the Purchase Order.

3.4. Measuring and Improving Predictive Scheduling Accuracy

There is a diagnostic tool to measure and improve the predictive accuracy of the Projected Schedule that I call the "Archery Chart". This approach can be understood by visualizing an archer aiming at a target. When his arrow hits the target, the distance of that the arrow deviates from the center bullseye represents the predictive error of the Projected Schedule. This aiming error increases with the archer's distance from the target. Obviously, the archer is lucky if he hits the target at a distance of 100 yards and the resulting error will be great. However, the aiming error decreases as he progressively steps closer to the target. In fact, the error should ideally go to zero when he is so close to the target that his nose is actually touching it! He should be able to hit a bullseye every single time when his distance from the target essentially equals zero.

Figure 10. Archery as a metaphor for measuring and improving the predictive accuracy of the Projected Schedule.

The accuracy of the Projected Schedule in predicting when jobs will be completed and ready to ship follows this archery metaphor. If you were in an aircraft factory on May 1st and asked the Projected Schedule to estimate when a specific aircraft will be completed, it might indicate an ECD of July 1st. If you then waited to see when the aircraft actually was completed, say on July 23rd, you would then conclude that the predictive error of the Projected Schedule, in this case, was approximately 3 weeks at a scheduling horizon of 52 days. I am defining the predictive error as the actual completion date minus the projected ECD, which is an indication of how overly optimistic the system's projection is. You could continue to record the projected ECDs for the aircraft's final assembly Production Order every day as time goes by to see how they evolve. In fact, you could set up an automated query to record the projected ECDs for all of the aircrafts' end-item Production Orders each day until they are actually completed and then record the actual completion dates for each aircraft. If you did this, you would be able to construct the graph shown in Figure 11 for a single aircraft showing the evolution of projected ECDs over time. The underlying dataset used to create this chart is shown in Table 2.

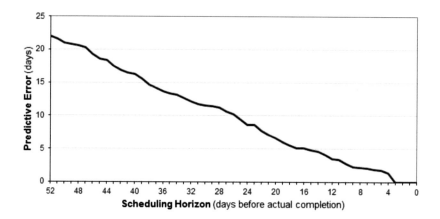

Figure 11. Example of an Archery Chart showing the evolution of projected ECDs for a single Production Order over time.

Table 2. Example of an Archery Chart dataset.

Observation Date	Num Days Before Actual Completion	Projected ECD	Actual Completion Date	Predictive Error (days)
6/1/2017	52	7/1/2017	7/23/2017	22
6/2/2017	51	7/1/2017	7/23/2017	22
6/3/2017	50	7/1/2017	7/23/2017	21
6/4/2017	49	7/2/2017	7/23/2017	21
6/5/2017	48	7/2/2017	7/23/2017	21
6/6/2017	47	7/2/2017	7/23/2017	20
6/7/2017	46	7/3/2017	7/23/2017	19
6/8/2017	45	7/4/2017	7/23/2017	19
6/9/2017	44	7/4/2017	7/23/2017	18
6/10/2017	43	7/5/2017	7/23/2017	18
6/11/2017	42	7/6/2017	7/23/2017	17
6/12/2017	41	7/6/2017	7/23/2017	16
6/13/2017	40	7/6/2017	7/23/2017	16
6/14/2017	39	7/7/2017	7/23/2017	16
6/15/2017	38	7/8/2017	7/23/2017	15
6/16/2017	37	7/8/2017	7/23/2017	14
6/17/2017	36	7/9/2017	7/23/2017	14
6/18/2017	35	7/9/2017	7/23/2017	13
6/19/2017	34	7/9/2017	7/23/2017	13
6/20/2017	33	7/10/2017	7/23/2017	13
6/21/2017	32	7/10/2017	7/23/2017	12
6/22/2017	31	7/11/2017	7/23/2017	12
6/23/2017	30	7/11/2017	7/23/2017	12
6/24/2017	29	7/11/2017	7/23/2017	11
6/25/2017	28	7/11/2017	7/23/2017	11
6/26/2017	27	7/12/2017	7/23/2017	11
6/27/2017	26	7/12/2017	7/23/2017	10
6/28/2017	25	7/13/2017	7/23/2017	9
6/29/2017	24	7/14/2017	7/23/2017	9
6/30/2017	23	7/14/2017	7/23/2017	9
7/1/2017	22	7/15/2017	7/23/2017	8
7/2/2017	21	7/15/2017	7/23/2017	7
7/3/2017	20	7/16/2017	7/23/2017	7
7/4/2017	19	7/17/2017	7/23/2017	6
7/5/2017	18	7/17/2017	7/23/2017	5
7/6/2017	17	7/17/2017	7/23/2017	5
7/7/2017	16	7/17/2017	7/23/2017	5
7/8/2017	15	7/18/2017	7/23/2017	5
7/9/2017	14	7/18/2017	7/23/2017	5
7/10/2017	13	7/18/2017	7/23/2017	4
7/11/2017	12	7/19/2017	7/23/2017	4
7/12/2017	11	7/19/2017	7/23/2017	3
7/13/2017	10	7/20/2017	7/23/2017	3
7/14/2017	9	7/20/2017	7/23/2017	2
7/15/2017	8	7/20/2017	7/23/2017	2
7/16/2017	7	7/20/2017	7/20/2017	2
7/17/2017	6	7/21/2017	7/23/2017	2
7/18/2017	5	7/21/2017	7/23/2017	2
7/19/2017	4	7/21/2017	7/23/2017	1
7/20/2017	3	7/22/2017	7/23/2017	0
7/21/2017	2	7/22/2017	7/23/2017	0
7/22/2017	1	7/23/2017	7/23/2017	0
7/23/2017	0	7/23/2017	7/23/2017	0

I warn you that this data may be a challenge to collect and harder still to display as a graphic chart. I don't suggest that you commit to manipulating this data on a routine basis but it will probably be useful to do this as a special project at least once to see what insights you might gain. The good news is that you only have to troubleshoot a couple of Production Orders to uncover some key root causes. It would be best to select only those Production Orders having Baseline Schedules that remained static throughout the period of observation. This is because we want to isolate the orders whose ECDs changed for some intrinsic reason and not because the customer revised his due date. Choose Production Orders for single parts rather than assemblies in order to keep the complexity manageable. Our aircraft example was just to illustrate the concept. Selecting a single strut, rib, or control rod would be more practical. Once you are able to systematically resolve a root cause source of error for a single Production Order, you will find that you probably will have eliminated the same source of error for dozens or hundreds of other active Production Orders as well as for thousands more yet to come!

In the Figure 11 example, we see that the predictive error decreases the nearer that we get to the actual completion date. It's as if the direction of the arrow's flight is from left to right. You may have noticed that I set up the horizontal axis in an unusual way with values decreasing as we go from left to right. The only reason for this is that I seem to believe that arrows always fly from left to right. That's all.

There are, in theory, many different ways these charts could look. For example, it is possible for some predictive errors to be negative as shown in Figure 12. Negative errors indicate that the system projected an order to be completed *later* than it *in fact* did. Note also, when viewing multiple Production Orders on the same chart, that the data for some Production Orders may be longer than others, as shown in this example. This is just because some Production Orders took longer to complete than others. You can also now appreciate our choice of displaying this data as a function of "days before actual completion" since it serves to normalize the data so that multiple Production Orders can neatly be displayed on top of each other on one chart. The value of this exercise is that we will use it as a way of looking at the Projected Schedule and troubleshooting it with the hope of giving product managers and customers better information.

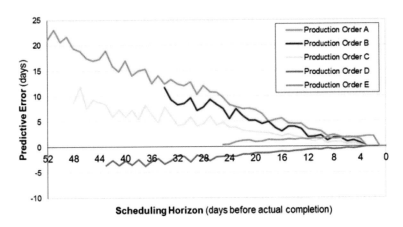

Figure 12. Example of an Archery Chart showing predictive error for five different Production Orders.

Now that you know what Archery Charts are and how to make them, what secrets can they reveal and what opportunities can they provide? In truth, the examples I have shown you so far are somewhat idealized for illustrative purposes. Let's therefore take a very close look at another example (Figure 13) that is more realistic and that you're more likely to see in practice. We will see that there are a few characteristic tell-tale artifacts that show up in these charts that can help point to where to look for sources of predictive error. Keep in mind that there are many, many possible sources of error some of which we will not always be able to ascertain from analyzing an Archery Chart. However, if there are material or labor transactional errors, we stand a good chance of noticing them from a rigorous post-mortem investigation informed by our Archery Chart.

You will see that these charts tend to consist of segmented lines that sometimes rise, sometimes fall, and sometimes stay flat. What do these artifacts tell us? Let's walk through them one at a time but remember, I'm going to use the horizontal axis convention as I did before in which values decrease as we go from left to right.

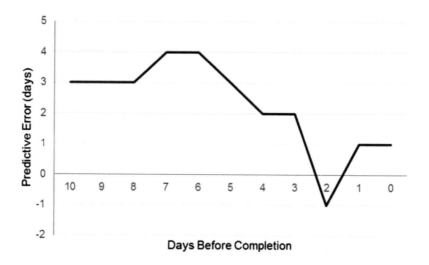

Figure 13. Realistic example of an Archery Chart.

A line segment that is rising from left to right means that the system accelerated the ECD (i.e., moved it to the left on the timeline). It's almost as if more work had been accomplished than was originally anticipated by the system. Here are a few possibilities as to why that might be:

- There were previous operations that were left open and then they were all closed at once. The rise occurred when the operations were closed retroactively.

- Operators closed an operation prematurely before it was actually finished
- A required material was issued to the Production Order earlier than expected
- Time standards (setup and run times) for the operation were over-estimated

- Work was accomplished faster than expected

If the predictive error was high to begin with, then there is a heightened need to understand what has made matters worse. You might need to pore through the labor tickets and material transactions as part of your investigation to find out what happened on the date that the rise occurred. This can be tedious and overwhelming. I suggest working from right to left when looking at Figure 13. In this example, we see that predictive errors existed near the end of the Production Order. It may therefore be easier to identify and resolve problems if you begin your forensic investigation with the final operations of the Production Order where the cumulative errors are less.

The second scenario is a predictive error line that stays flat indicating that the ECD is unchanged from the previous day. This actually a very good thing because it suggests that the scheduling engine is keeping pace with the actual work done. It's reflecting a case of accomplishing one full day's work with each passing day. Isn't that exactly what we would want? You can convince yourself of this interpretation by considering the ideal case of a job whose Projected Schedule estimated the final ECD with perfect accuracy: It's a flat line that coincides with the horizontal axis and is perfectly flat at every point.

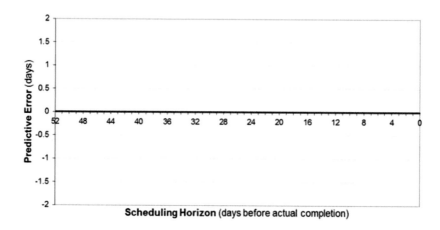

Figure 14. Idealized Archery Chart for a perfectly predictive Projected Schedule.

The third scenario is a falling line. A slope that is less than or equal to -1 gives the appearance of less progress being made than expected. Possible causes include:

- Operators are not performing labor transactions

- Required materials are getting issued late or not at all

- The time standards (setup and run times) for the operation were under-estimated

- Engineering change or quality non-conformance delays have been incurred.

Table 3 summarizes the three archetypes we have just discussed and shows some sample dates to help visualize how projected ECDs, predictive errors, and Archery Charts relate to each other.

Table 3. Archery Chart archetypes.

Rising:

(Slope ≥ 1)
Appears that more work has
been done than expected.

Days Before Act. Completion	Projected ECD	Act. Completion Date	Predictive Error (days)
6	7/12/2017	7/12/2017	0
5	7/11/2017	7/12/2017	1
4	7/9/2017	7/12/2017	3

Flat:

(Slope =0)
System keeping pace with
actual work done

Days Before Act. Completion	Projected ECD	Act. Completion Date	Predictive Error (days)
6	7/12/2017	7/12/2017	0
5	7/12/2017	7/12/2017	0
4	7/12/2017	7/12/2017	0

Falling:

(Slope ≤ -1)
Appears that less work has
been done than expected.

Days Before Act. Completion	Projected ECD	Act. Completion Date	Predictive Error (days)
6	7/12/2017	7/12/2017	0
5	7/13/2017	7/12/2017	-1
4	7/15/2017	7/12/2017	-3

3.5. Capacity Schedule: Resource Planning Tool

The Capacity Schedule is different from the other three schedules in that it is not intended as a tool for managing daily operations. It is rather a capacity management tool useful for periodic management reviews intended to ensure that the amount of available manufacturing capacity is well aligned with current and forecasted customer demand. Many of you will recognize this as the central aim of Sales, Inventory, and Operations Planning (SIOP). SIOP is a formal management process that has gained increased notoriety among corporate consultants and managers and has been instituted as a central element of many business' strategic management process.

The Capacity Schedule generated by the ERP or APS scheduling engine brings together the following two considerations: 1) The manufacturing load imposed by current and future customer orders; and 2) the current capacity available at each manufacturing work center or resource. These considerations can be realized by establishing a separate "what-if" Capacity Schedule that is a backwards infinite-capacity schedule. The assumption of infinite capacity here is essential since we want the system to show us how overloaded each work center is based on customers' due date requirements. Imposing finite capacity in the Capacity Schedule would prevent loads from exceeding 100% of capacity, which is exactly what we don't want. We instead want loads to naturally fall above or below the 100% line consistent with the level of customer demand without any remedial intervention.

There is also the question of how to deal with past due manufacturing backlog in the Capacity Schedule. Many manufacturers may be facing the situation depicted in Figure 15 where a past-due backlog dominates at the current dateline and is continually pushed forward as time advances. Note that this graphic illustrates a forward schedule, not a backwards schedule as was just prescribed above. The issue is what kind of Capacity Schedule best informs capital and human resource planning? If the backlog is relatively minor, then a backwards Capacity Schedule places manufacturing load on the timeline consistent with customer demand. In the example of Figure 15, this would mean that past-due manufacturing loads would be allowed to flow into the past. Load vs. capacity metrics based on such a schedule would objectively show where load stands relative to available capacity, therefore best supporting capital and staffing decisions. If, however, the backlog is large, then a forwards Capacity Schedule offers a more realistic picture. It may be useful to run the Capacity Schedule both ways in order to provide both views so that capital equipment and human resource investment decisions can be objectively made.

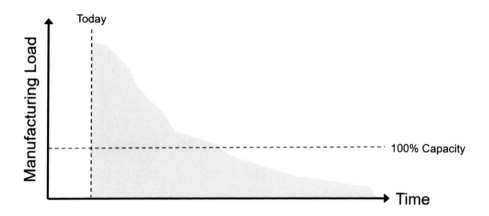

Figure 15. Significant overcapacity situation caused by past-due backlog.

There are various strategies and techniques to work yourself out of a large backlog. One of the most important near-term strategies when faced with this challenge is to review new customer orders to initially ensure feasible customer due dates as described in Chapters 3.1 and 5.1 in the light of available capacity. If this were done for the situation shown in Figure 15, new customer orders would only be accepted far enough in the future when sufficient available capacity exists to realistically fulfill the order. This approach can be extremely helpful because continuing to accept new orders while ignoring capacity overloads will only exacerbate the situation and perpetuate past due orders.

3.6. *Overcoming System Limitations*

There is undoubtedly a multitude of issues you will encounter when implementing and managing an ERP, MRP, or APS system. Some of those issues will be born out of system limitations. There may be alternative yet equivalent (or nearly equivalent) approaches you can take or workarounds that can be employed. The Dispatch List is a good example of a workaround since it is something that systems don't offer out-of-the-box and is therefore something you must build yourself.

With the sheer number of available systems, it is impossible to prescribe within these pages a corrective solution for any particular challenge. You can feel free to contact me with questions as to how to best proceed if you encounter issues that are particularly challenging or critical. My email and website are shown in the About the Author section near the beginning of this book. However, in general, one thing I can recommend is to have a way to develop and execute Structured Query Language (SQL) queries directly in the backend database. This is not only essential to overcoming system limitations, it will come in very handy for effectively managing the master data in the system as well as establishing static, real-time, and near-real-time reporting either inside or outside of the system. It is therefore important either to be able to do this yourself or have someone available to you internally or externally that understands your systems and can bridge the gap between business objectives and IT. I have found this capability to be critical and indispensable, which tends to go beyond just programming.

4. Establishing and Delivering Lean Shop Floor Signals

4.1. Developing Real-Time Dispatch Lists

Now for the star of our show: The Dispatch List! In Chapter 1, we introduced the idea of the need for a *regulatory mechanism* to mediate Lean material flow. What that means is that we need a visual signal that tells us when the next work center in a routing is ready to take in new work. As you recall from Section 2.2, we are modelling each work center as a one-bin kanban having kanban quantity, K:

$$K = \mu L + N\sqrt{L}\sigma$$

This means that each work center is bound not to exceed this critical quantity in the interest of maintaining Lean flow.

However, here is where we need to make a fundamental adjustment so that our one-bin kanban can function in the context of multiple part numbers flowing through each work center. Keeping track of product *quantities* is obviously inadequate because not all parts are created equal. Some parts involve only a few man-hours (or machine-hours) of work whereas others may require dozens of man-hours. We therefore need to consider the capacity of the one-bin kanban using units of work rather than units of quantity. Work is therefore the "common denominator" that will allow us to broadly apply our kanban model to all work centers for all products.

Our work center model now becomes:

$$W = \mu + N\sigma$$

where W represents the not-to-exceed work center daily capacity measured in units of work (i.e., man-hours or machine-hours). As we have it now, W is a function of the average (μ) and standard deviation (σ) of daily demand also both expressed in the same work units. We eliminated L by considering a period of one day such that $L = 1$. N remains as a safety factor to account for demand variations (usually between 0.1 and 0.8 for work centers that can support multiple simultaneous jobs or 1 to 3 for work centers limited to one job at a time). Note that when we say "demand", we are referring to the demand imposed on the work center of interest by all immediately downstream work centers and products. This is problematic because of the multiplicity of output streams. We could resolve this by integrating over all output streams to calculate effective values for μ and σ but I'm going to avoid doing that by introducing some simplifying assumptions.

The first step is to redefine the above expression by assuming that the sum of all demands is roughly equivalent to the productive daily capacity of the work center:

$$P \approx \sum_{i=1}^{n} \mu_i$$

so that

$$W = P + N\sigma$$

This is a reasonable assumption if the factory is "right-sized". At worst, P may be greater than the sum of demands (i.e., we have excess capacity). The implication of having overcapacity is that we may end up with greater than optimum WIP inventory at that work center.

Our second step is to eliminate the need for σ by recognizing that the purpose of the second term, $N\sigma$, is simply to provide a buffer to absorb fluctuating demand. It is, in essence, a "fudge factor". Therefore, we can end up with the following expression that fulfills these same functions and provides us with a practical and effective approach to defining "one-bin kanban" work centers:

$$W = AP(1 + N)$$

The new variable, A, is a multiplicative scaling factor. Remember, we assumed production capacity for one day (P). For a one-shift operation we might consider one day equal to eight hours. We would then want to set the scaling factor, A, to 50% if the *average* working time for jobs at the work center is around four hours. The physical interpretation of this expression is straightforward: The first term AP is the work center's effective production capacity and the second term APN is it's buffer capacity.

Note that there is an alternative and more simplified embodiment of this one-bin Kanban approach that can be practiced with systems where the capacity of each work center is defined by the maximum number of jobs that can be worked on simultaneously. Some systems tacitly assume that only one job can be worked at a time whereas others allow the maximum number of simultaneous jobs to be specified for each work center. This differs from the "bucket-of-available-hours" capacity model we have developed so far. For systems where the maximum number of simultaneous jobs (let's call it C_{max}) is specified, we can use this alternative expression to represent work center capacity:

$$W = C_{max}(1 + N)$$

Let's now think about how this approach will actually be applied on the shop floor. To visualize the work flow, consider three work centers in series (1, 2, and 3) as shown in Figure 16 each with the following attributes all expressed in units of "resource hours" where the resource may either be men or machines.

$$[AP]_1 = 9$$
$$[AP(1 + N)]_1 = 12$$
$$[AP]_2 = 12$$
$$[AP(1 + N)]_2 = 15$$
$$[AP]_1 = 9$$
$$[AP(1 + N)]_1 = 12$$

As a simplification, each white circle represents a unit of available capacity and each solid red circle represents an equal unit of workload in each work center.

You will see that we've subdivided each work center into two areas: A *Production Area* and an *Outgoing Area*. These can and should be areas physically identified within each work center. We will find these two areas helpful for visualizing how our regulatory mechanism actually works in practice. We will also apply this idea of two areas later when constructing our Dispatch Lists.

The Production Area essentially represents available production capacity. Ideally it should not contain any idle jobs as it represents work center capacity that is ready and available to do work. The Outgoing Area is where completed jobs wait until the next work center is ready to accept them. It, in contrast, is composed entirely of idle work. We could eliminate the Outgoing Area entirely by setting N to zero. This would be perfectly fine if the sequential work centers' production rates were in fact all balanced (i.e., equal) and demand remained constant such that one-piece flow was prevalent. In real-world practice, however, both demand and production rates fluctuate and so some kind of buffer Is appropriate just as it would be if we were working with physical kanbans.

Let's consider the scenario labelled "Frame 1" in Figure 16 and take it as our starting point. This is a simple one-dimensional model but it should be effective in illustrating the mechanics of the system. We will later extrapolate this model to one where there are multiple output streams. In this model, we see that Work Center 3 is full and cannot accept any new work. Moving upstream, Work Center 2 has three completed units lying idle in the Outgoing Area until production capacity becomes available in Work Center 3.

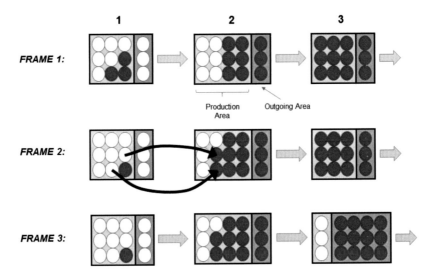

Figure 16. Example of mediated Lean material flow between three work centers.

The criteria for being able to move work to the next work center has two parts that must both be satisfied:

$$\begin{cases} W_{work\ center} < AP(1+N) \\ W_{in\ production} < AP \end{cases}$$

which says that work can be moved forward whenever the actual total amount of work present at next work center, $W_{work\ center}$, falls below its critical kanban quantity *and* there is production capacity available to absorb it. The maximum amount of work that can then be moved to this work center is:

$$W_{move} = min \begin{cases} AP(1 + N) - W_{work\ center} \\ AP - W_{in\ production} \end{cases}$$

where the right hand side is evaluated at each downstream work center. If work is completed but this move condition cannot be satisfied, then it is held in the current work center's outgoing queue until capacity is freed downstream.

As time moves on, we see that the "Frame 2" scenario involves two units in Work Center 1 being completed in production and immediately getting moved to Work Center 2 where there is available capacity.

Finally, "Frame 3" is where we practice the virtue of honorable restraint. In "Frame 3", Work Center 3 has completed enough work to fill its outgoing area with the full *AP(1 + N)* quantity. Although there are three completed units in the Outgoing Area of Work Center 2, they are not moved forward to Work Center 3 because the move condition is not satisfied despite there being available production capacity in Work Center 3. Holding on to completed work in this way has the effect of propagating information upstream to controllably throttle material flow commensurate with a pull system. Material will continue to be held at Work Center 2 until Work Center 3 is able to relieve its workload so that all work can move forward.

Now let's extrapolate this pull mechanism to the multi-dimensional scenario illustrated in Figure 17. Here we see that the blue and red products cannot move forward because their corresponding downstream work centers are full. However, the yellow product in Work Center 1, once completed, will immediately satisfy the move condition and will be moved to Work Center 2 unaffected by the adjacent log jams at Work Centers 3 and 4.

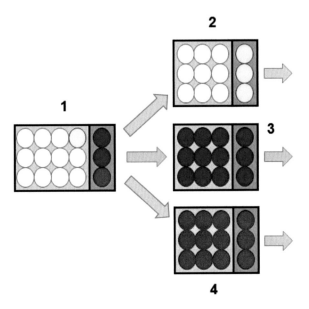

Figure 17. Work center example with multiple outputs.

We have now gotten a glimpse into the detailed mechanics of how a Lean pull system can be realized in a job shop environment as part of a comprehensive and scalable production control strategy. Prerequisites for ensuring the viability of employing this approach are summarized as follows:

1. Work Center calendars must be validated to ensure that they accurately and effectively provide nominal work center capacities

2. Production routings (a.k.a. bills of operations) must contain valid setup and run times so that the load imposed on any work center can be accurately estimated.

3. Labor transactions must be timely and accurate so that the work that lie in each work center can be accurately known.

4. A good Dispatch List is needed that signals operators when it is OK to move jobs forward.

Section 6.1 describes an employee training method that vividly demonstrates how the Dispatch List works and how it is able to drive improved shop floor performance. I encourage readers to work through Section 6.1 to get immersive exposure to the detailed mechanics of this approach.

So what does a Dispatch List look like? Figure 18 provides a simple example that shows the essential design elements. Firstly, all the job operations on this list are operations that are physically located in one work center, the MACHNG06 work center in this example. This means that each work center should have its own electronic Dispatch List dynamically connected to the system to provide near-real-time signals. The list is also divided into two sections: The Production Area operations are in the top half of the list and the Outgoing Area operations are shown in the bottom half of the list. As soon as an operation is completed, it is moved from the Production section to the Outgoing section with an action message instructing the operator to either hold or move the work.

The first column prioritizes the work. You will notice in this Figure 18 example that the highest priority jobs (1, 2, and 3) were worked first and they are therefore the first ones ready to be moved to the next work center. There are many ways to prioritize work but prioritizing by the Baseline operation start or finish (due) date are straightforward and effective approaches for maximizing on-time performance. Prioritizing by the operation due date is referred to as the Earliest Due Date (EDD) rule, which serves to minimize the maximum lateness of all jobs. It is a popular, easy, and effective approach to implement. Much of this data can be obtained or derived directly from MES (manufacturing execution system) data.

There is another prioritization technique based on "buffer penetration" that also maximizes on-time completions, but in a risk-adjusted way. I only mention it here for reference. The point is that you can prioritize the jobs any way you want using baseline schedule dates but prioritizing on the basis of the operation due date, operation start date, or (if you want to get fancy) buffer penetration will most often lead to better results.

Work Center:

MACHNG06, MACHINING, 5-AXIS

Priority:	Job ID:	Oper:	Status:
4	10023	40	Running
5	10033	40	Running
6	10037	40	Running
7	10045	40	Idle
8	10052	30	Running
9	10061	45	Running
10	10071	30	Running
11	10075	40	Idle
12	10079	40	Running

Outgoing:			
1	10087	40	**Move to CLEANG01**
2	10090	30	Hold for DEBUR02
3	10096	45	Hold for DEBUR02

Figure 18. Dispatch List example.

Did you notice that this Dispatch List example doesn't show schedule dates? Heresy! I left them off intentionally to emphasize the idea that the order in which work is done can be one of the biggest factors affecting overall on-time performance. Feel free to approach this differently if you think it will provide meaningful benefits. Adding dates to the Dispatch Lists is perfectly reasonable. However, my only caution is that providing dates can lead to a diversity of approaches being practiced on the shop floor. Operators, expeditors, dispatchers, supervisors, project managers, "schedulers", and virtually anyone who is trying to do "the right thing" may use published dates in their own special way such that different work centers end up using different logic to sequence and prioritize work. This can lead to a lack of coordination between different parts of the factory. Large assemblies are often the most visible causalities of this approach in which components and subassemblies don't come together at the right time. Coordinating the entire factory using priorities derived from a centrally-managed customer-driven Baseline Schedule, even an imperfect one, at the very least provides uniformity and coordination achieved through a common drum beat.

You might say that Figure 18 is somewhat idealized (although not necessarily unrealistic) in that the operations all appear to have been worked in exactly the correct priority order. This is indeed the way a Dispatch List should look. However, Figure 19 shows a different scenario in which priorities 4, 5, & 9 where completed prematurely and therefore appear out-of-sequence on the list.

Work Center:
MACHNG06, MACHINING, 5-AXIS

Priority:	Job ID:	Oper:	Status:
1	10023	40	Running
2	10033	40	Running
3	10037	40	Running
6	10045	40	Idle
7	10052	30	Running
8	10061	45	Running
10	10079	40	Running
11	10087	40	Running
12	10090	30	Running

Outgoing:

4	10071	30	**Move to CLEANG01**
5	10075	40	Hold for DEBUR02
9	10096	45	Hold for DEBUR02

Figure 19. Example Dispatch List showing out-of-sequence work.

A complicating issue is the batching of similar jobs to minimize total setup time. Multiple jobs sharing the same setup can provide a significant lead time and cost advantage when setup times are significant. Some APS systems provide sophisticated functionality to group similar jobs and schedule them together. If that is the case, our Dispatch List design will do just fine since batched jobs will be automatically grouped together on the list. However, if you do not have this APS functionality, then a manual workaround is possible.

This workaround involves the operators searching for similar "batchable" jobs on the Dispatch List whenever they reach a job where batching is appropriate. In this scenario, a shop floor policy is established that allows jobs to be worked early if and only if they can be batched with the current job *and* they are scheduled within a prescribed maximum allowable time horizon. The idea of a maximum allowable time horizon is an important one because it prevents jobs due today and jobs due six months from now from being unreasonably batched together. You may, for example, set the maximum allowable time horizon to allow jobs to be batched if they are scheduled to run within the next five days. This would be a case where displaying the Baseline Schedule dates on the Dispatch List would be useful.

4.2. Using Metrics to Monitor Execution

There are an enormous number of metrics we could contemplate, but let's just focus on those metrics that lend themselves directly to driving schedule performance. That means we are going to put aside quality and cost metrics as they are outside our main scope.

As with many things, overall schedule performance depends on doing a large number of small things right. We will therefore consider metrics in two categories: 1) Top level schedule performance metrics and 2) lower level executional metrics. The top-level metrics are commonly practiced but we'll try to take a step back to make sure we're getting an effective view of overall schedule performance. The lower level executional metrics I will present are not commonly practiced and so I will spend some extra time explaining what they are and what they're good for.

To begin our survey of schedule metrics, let's look at the top-level schedule performance metrics, which are the ones many of us have seen before. Here are a handful of examples of top level metrics that address schedule performance at different levels and stages of production:

Sales Order Level:

- % on-time shipments
- Early/late shipment aging
- On-time shipping trend

End-Item Job Level:

- % on-time end-item job completions
- Early/late end-item job completion aging
- On-time end-Item job completion trend

Job Level (all jobs)**:**

- % on-time job completions
- Early/late job completion aging
- On-time job completion trend

Job Operation Level:

- % on-time job operation completions
- Early/late job operation aging
- On-time operation completion trend

As you can see, each group of metrics consists of three different views: A static snapshot, a distribution of outcomes, and a trend over time. Each of these views is really measuring the same thing but in different ways. This is an approach we can generally take with all metrics, not just those having to do with schedule performance.

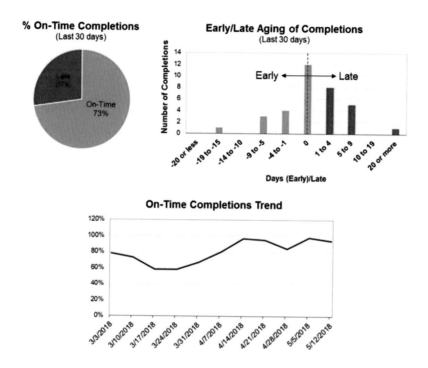

Figure 20. Top level schedule performance metric examples.

A generally accepted good practice is to limit the use of metrics to only those few that are most important – typically no more than five. So when it comes to top level schedule performance metrics, my preference is to focus on the final outcome, which for the manufacturing organization is the completion of the end-item job (i.e., end-item Production Order) and individual job operation completions. Someone in the company should always keep an eye on on-time shipping performance, which is obviously important since it has a very direct connection to customer satisfaction. In this book, however, we are focused on monitoring the health and effectiveness of the manufacturing function, so we will put on-time shipping aside for this discussion.

We should also be interested in looking at schedule performance at the operation level just as we did for the end items. I tend to put less weight on measuring job level outcomes because they are not sufficiently granular enough to point out where problems lie in the production process. After all, a Production Order depends on all its individual operations being completed on time. This operation level approach allows us to measure schedule performance by work center, which is essential for capacity planning and knowing where bottlenecks exist.

An exception is to consider job level on-time performance if there are a handful of major sub-assemblies that represent critical branches of the value chain. For example, it might be useful to track schedule performance not just for the completion of each aircraft but also for the major sections of each aircraft (e.g., aft fuselage, wing structure, engine installation, etc.).

Figure 21 and Figure 22 summarize a suggested approach to top level schedule performance metrics. Note that Figure 21 shows a dashboard example that includes a drop-down list allowing the user to view end-item schedule performance either for a single product line or the entire factory. You could also construct the same kind of dashboard to measure on-time performance by work center. In this case, the drop-down list would allow you to switch between individual work centers. Figure 22 does exactly this but it is presented more as a one-page summary of work center performance so that you don't have to switch between work centers.

Note that the work centers are listed in Figure 22 roughly in the same order that production proceeds. The color coding gives us a quick way to see if on-time performance is dropping off precipitously at certain work centers thus indicating the possibility of bottlenecks. We can take this same data and plot it out as shown in Figure 23 transforming it from a tabular to a graphic view. Here we can see clearly that schedule performance tends to degrade most significantly early on in the machining areas

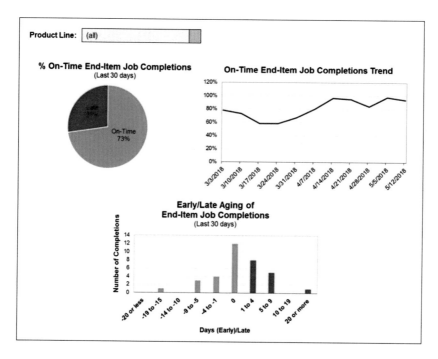

Figure 21. Top level schedule metrics for end-item jobs.

Work Center	% On-Time Ops	Avg Days Late	Max Days Late
MATL	94%	2	2
CUTTNG01	95%	2	9
MACHNG01	91%	1	6
MACHNG02	85%	3	3
MACHNG03	79%	3	5
TURNG01	80%	2	2
EDM01	78%	4	11
EDM02	78%	3	3
DEBURR01	76%	3	8
CLEANG01	75%	4	10
ANOD01	75%	4	12
ADHES01	78%	3	5
ADHES02	75%	2	6
WELDNG01	73%	2	7
ASSY01	69%	3	5
ASSY02	72%	4	11
ASSY03	75%	4	7
PACK01	70%	4	5
SHPPNG	65%	6	12

Figure 22. Top level on-time operations by work center.

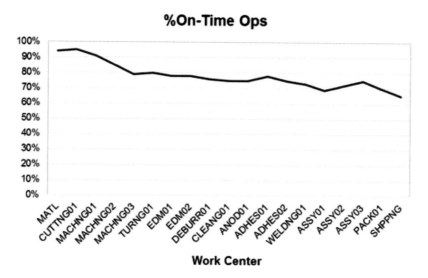

Figure 23. Example of schedule performance degrading as products advance through the production process.

We began our look at schedule performance metrics by considering top level metrics that evaluate work completion outcomes. Viewing this data by work center allowed us to identify areas of interest where schedule performance problems are visible. We can now to drill into these problem areas to uncover possible solutions by thinking about what it takes to achieve on-time completions.

In general, we can say that on-time performance nominally depends on satisfying three conditions:

- The operation must start on time
- Work must be completed consistent with the time allotted in the Baseline Schedule (i.e., total actual cycle time must be

less than or equal to total cycle time planned for the operation)

- The operation must finish on time

The third condition can be discarded because it represents the final outcome for the operation that we are trying to work towards. We instead want to focus on the executional aspects that lead either positively or negatively to achieving these outcomes. Let's unpack the first condition a little bit. An operation can start on time if:

- Preceding operations are completed on time such that the work center does not inherit work that was already late
- Jobs are worked in a sequential order that supports on-time starts
- Sufficient work center capacity is available to accept the job on time

One of the main ideas of this book is the assertion that we can improve the overall performance of the factory by improving the performance of individual work centers. Indeed, if each work center operated in an optimum way, then each work center would pass work downstream on time and no work center would inherit late work. This is exactly the kind of self-fulfilling prophecy we want to realize. We are therefore left with the last two conditions listed above as being those that are most relevant to starting operations on time.

Now we need to address what is required to actually perform the work with a duration that is consistent with the Baseline Schedule. The ability of performing work within the allotted time can be measured by evaluating *labor efficiency* for each work center. This is a common metric that most of you are already be familiar with. It is simply the baseline time standard for the operation divided by the actual work hours:

$$efficiency = \frac{T_{setup} + N_{completed}T_{run}}{t_{setup} + N_{completed}t_{run}}$$

where T_{setup} and T_{run} are the baseline setup and run time standards defined in the manufacturing routings, t_{setup} and t_{run} are the actual setup and run times recorded through the labor collection system, and $N_{completed}$ is the quantity of products worked on. Note that this expression for efficiency is most accurately evaluated after the operation has been completed so as not to overweight the role of setup. We can see that if setup and run for an operation are expected to take a total of two hours (in the numerator) but it actually takes four hours (in the denominator), then the overall efficiency is 50%.

The notion of efficiency is, of course, relative to the Baseline Schedule. If the Baseline Schedule plans a simple cleaning operation to last an inordinate amount of time, say 900 hours, then a 900-hour cleaning operation will be viewed as being 100% efficient. We can then question whether our baseline estimates are appropriate. If shop floor supervision is effective in moving work along at a reasonable pace, then we can rely on efficiency metrics to point out where our time standards are out of whack. We will either see consistently very high or very low efficiencies in a certain area, which will stick out like a sore thumb leading us to update certain time standards.

An important thing to keep in mind when calculating labor efficiency metrics is that we are not literally dividing hours by hours to get a dimensionless figure of merit. The labor collection system will necessarily be providing us with *man-hours*, which is really a unit of work, not time. This is not an issue mathematically if all our operations each require only one operator working at a time. However, we will need to take extra care in defining the baseline time standards if any operation in our factory requires more than one person working simultaneously. Defining simultaneous resource requirements within the manufacturing routings is something that not all ERP systems do.

Whatever the capabilities of your ERP system may be, the setup and run portions of an operation really need to satisfy two aims: They need to convey duration of the work (in hours) for schedule calculation purposes and work content (in man-hours, machine-hours, or, more generically, resource-hours) for efficiency metric calculation purposes. You should look for ways that your system supports the definition of simultaneous work center resources within each manufacturing operation. An outside-the-system workaround for efficiency calculation will be needed if your system does not directly support this.

As we mentioned at the outset, quality is another an essential prerequisite for meeting schedule objectives. For that reason, measuring the defect rate prevalent in each work center is often a valuable thing to do. A good way to do it is to divide the number of in-process defects found over a fixed period by the number of man-hours over that same period. This metric usually normalized further by expressing it as "defects per 1000 man-hours".

At this point, we have deconstructed what is needed to attain on-time performance and can finally summarize it as follows:

- Jobs are worked in a sequential order that enables on-time starts

  (i.e., priorities are being followed)

- Sufficient work center capacity is available to accept the job on time

  (i.e., manufacturing capacity is being managed effectively)

- The operations must be performed with a duration consistent with Baseline Schedule

  (i.e., labor efficiency must be near 100% or greater)

- Quality levels must be high

  (i.e., defects/1000 man-hours is low)

These four requirements are then what we should focus on as we develop lower level executional metrics. We focus on these four things because they form the essential prerequisites for schedule adherence. We have already addressed the third point in some detail concerning efficiency measurement, so let's address the first two points concerning work priorities and manufacturing capacity.

Measuring adherence to work priorities is something we will spend some extra time on as it is not often something that is commonly practiced. As I mentioned before, I view adherence to work priorities as an important prerequisite for on-time completions.

We can then define our priority adherence metric as the coefficient of correlation between the columns of actual and planned priorities. Excel provides a convenient CORREL function, which calculates the Pearson Product-Moment coefficient of correlation. In this example, we can use the CORREL function to get an adherence-to-priority correlation coefficient of 0.74. In general, we want to enforce adherence to priorities in a way that maximizes this metric for each work center Of course, the metric can be negatively affected when work is batched using the manual workaround we described earlier. We can either decide to accept this and take the metric with a grain of salt or we can take steps to precisely account for and correct this phenomenon in the metric calculation (not trivial).

Table 4 shows us a way to assess priority adherence by comparing the actual priorities taken on the shop floor with the priorities prescribed by the Baseline Schedule.

We can then define our priority adherence metric as the coefficient of correlation between the columns of actual and planned priorities. Excel provides a convenient CORREL function, which calculates the Pearson Product-Moment coefficient of correlation. In this example, we can use the CORREL function to get an adherence-to-priority correlation coefficient of 0.74. In general, we want to enforce adherence to priorities in a way that maximizes this metric for each work center. Of course, the metric can be negatively affected when work is batched using the manual workaround we described earlier. We can either decide to accept this and take the metric with a grain of salt or we can take steps to precisely account for and correct this phenomenon in the metric calculation (not trivial).

Table 4. Historical execution data to support priority adherence metrics.

Job	Op	Planned Priority	Baseline Start Date	Actual Priority	Actual Start Date
100012	50	1	1/3/2018	1	1/3/2018
100014	50	2	1/12/2018	2	1/13/2018
100023	55	3	1/24/2018	5	2/5/2018
100043	60	4	2/1/2018	6	2/6/2108
100052	40	5	2/5/2018	3	1/14/2018
100061	50	6	2/8/2018	7	2/12/2018
100062	45	7	2/9/2018	4	1/24/2018
100071	40	8	2/11/2018	8	2/13/2018

When it comes to evaluating manufacturing capacity, it is important to acknowledge that any evaluation of whether there is sufficient capacity necessarily requires the evaluation of shop load. Although this is widely understood, the terminology that people use often never mentions the term "load". As a result, charts and reports that claim to show "capacity" usually are really showing "load versus capacity". "Load versus capacity" is what we really need to know if we intend to improve schedule performance. We would know we had a problem if load exceeded capacity (i.e., load/capacity > 100%). In fact, it is usually wise to provide some "headroom" such that we raise a red flag if load/capacity is greater than, say, 85%.

Fortunately, most systems readily provide work center load versus capacity reporting. However, users must take care to ensure that these reports utilize Projected Schedule data rather than Baseline Schedule data. This is because the Projected Schedule is reflecting what work is actually present in the work centers today and what load is likely to exist in the future. Remember, the Projected Schedule is supposed to be predictive. The Baseline Schedule, on the other hand, is reflective only of what load was theoretically planned to exist. We want to understand load versus capacity as it transpires in reality, not as it was planned hypothetically. For that reason, the use of the Projected Schedule for capacity planning is required.

Table 5 now represents a basic yet comprehensive set of metrics for monitoring and resolving schedule performance by work center. The first three columns give us a top-level sense of schedule outcomes and the last four columns provide important lower level executional metrics that highlight the critical prerequisites necessary for on-time completions. If we see that a particular work center tends to suffer from poor on-time performance, then we only need to look to the last four columns of Table 5 to infer why that might be so we can begin attacking root causes. Adding a trend chart to any of these metrics would clearly show whether performance is improving or not. A trend chart of one or two of the most critical metrics posted at each work center is one of the best ways to provide supervisors and operators with valuable information that lets them know how they're doing. Providing this kind of public information is an excellent way to drive a shop floor culture that takes ownership of its performance and works to improve it.

There may be, of course, other external factors that can impact schedule performance. Mid-stream engineering changes or employee absences, for example, can throw a wrench into the manufacturing process. You may feel a need to expand Table 5 to address any other extenuating circumstances that might uniquely apply to your operation.

Table 5. Last four columns to show lower level executional metrics.

Work Center	% On-Time Ops	Avg Days Late	Max Days Late	Priority Adherence	Efficiency	Defects/ 1000-manhrs	Load/Capacity
MATL	94%	2	2	0.95	99%	1.4	103%
CUTTNG01	95%	2	9	0.80	84%	6.8	84%
MACHNG01	91%	1	6	0.67	77%	0.2	94%
MACHNG02	85%	3	3	0.70	84%	5.9	98%
MACHNG03	79%	3	5	0.75	88%	5.2	88%
TURNG01	80%	2	2	0.83	69%	3.3	78%
EDM01	78%	4	11	0.76	95%	3.7	78%
EDM02	78%	3	3	0.74	69%	3.7	60%
DEBURR01	76%	3	8	0.99	86%	4.6	80%
CLEANG01	75%	4	10	.82	62%	4.8	87%
ANOD01	75%	4	12	0.80	72%	0.0	70%
ADHES01	78%	3	5	0.92	101%	1.7	56%
ADHES02	75%	2	6	1.00	63%	4.9	70%
WELDNG01	73%	2	7	0.63	80%	0.5	55%
ASSY01	69%	3	5	0.80	65%	3.6	61%
ASSY02	72%	4	11	0.84	76%	6.9	51%
ASSY03	75%	4	7	0.82	63%	3.5	67%
PACK01	70%	4	5	0.90	114%	3.2	81%
SHPPNG	65%	6	12	0.98	114%	5.5	81%

5. Promoting Schedule Stability Through Effective Demand Planning

---

5.1. Customer Order Review and Acceptance

Although we have taken significant steps to ensure the intrinsic stability of the Baseline Schedule, external customers can inadvertently throw a wrench into the works in two ways: 1) the customer's schedule requirements can be outside our capabilities to deliver and therefore infeasible, and 2) the customer can request schedule changes that are feasible but are nevertheless undesirable because they induce volatility in the Baseline Schedule. This section outlines the use of a formal customer review and acceptance process as a safeguard against infeasible Customer Orders. The next section will lay out some rules of engagement that govern when schedule changes are appropriate.

Customer Order review and acceptance is something that should be performed when a customer submits a new or revised order. The objectives of this review include:

- Evaluating the order for schedule feasibility

- Evaluating the order for technical feasibility and manufacturability

- Validating customers' quality requirements and verifying the company's ability to meet them

- Ensuring correct pricing

This is principally a book about scheduling and production control so we will focus only on the first objective. The end goal is to either acknowledge to the customer that their order has been accepted as-is or reply to the customer with a proposed "best-we-can-do" due date that will hopefully be acceptable. Determining a feasible due date may be an iterative process.

You will recall that Section 3.1 described new Customer Orders being entered into the system and subsequently driving an exploded set of Production Orders in a planned state. What's important is that those planned Production Orders should be evaluated in the Projected Schedule. Our aim is to test whether the customer's desired due date is achievable. The Projected Schedule, being a forward schedule whose aim is to be predictive, is best able to indicate whether the customer's due date can realistically be met in the light of current shop floor loading. If it can, we can then firm the Production Orders in the Baseline Schedule for subsequent execution.

One approach for the Customer Order schedule review process is:

1. Enter the new Customer Order into ERP/MRP managing its dates as described in Section 6.2

2. Explode the Customer Order into its requisite set of Production Orders within the Projected Schedule. Leave the Production Orders in a planned state so their dates can be free to move.

3. Run the Projected Schedule

4. Does the projected finish date for the top-level Production Order meet the Customer Order's internal due date? You can accept the customer's proposed due date if it does. If it does not, then the projected finish date for the top-level Production Order is a more realistic completion date that you can propose to the customer.

5.2. Re-Baselining Policies

Some may perceive the need to change Customer Order due dates either because the customer has requested a change or the company sees that it is not able to fulfill an order on time. It is usually a customer-facing part of the organization such as Sales or Program Management that negotiates these changes. As was mentioned in the Introduction, Manufacturing is often a large ship that is slow to turn. Ideally, the feasibility of customer-directed changes should be formally assessed just as they were when the

Customer Order was initially accepted. Steps should also be taken to discourage the frequency of these changes so not to induce undesirable schedule volatility that could affect the company's ability to serve other customers. Similarly, internally-directed schedule changes should also be rigorously restricted for all but a few special cases, which have been determined to be acceptable by the company.

For these reasons, it is important for the company to have a written policy that governs when it is acceptable for the Baseline Schedule to be revised – that is, it needs a *re-baselining policy*. A written policy encourages self-discipline. Manufacturing companies that are fortunate enough to have a large number of customers will very likely have a significant fraction of those customers who themselves suffer from internal schedule volatility. Any firm that is part of an external supply chain will be at risk of having their Baseline Schedule disturbed by customer-induced schedule volatility unless steps are taken to deal with it equitably. Hidden costs can be incurred when this type of volatility is allowed to impact the firm's ability to function efficiently.

External customers aside, there may be some within the company who desire for the schedule to be re-baselined whenever Manufacturing cannot meet its original schedule commitments. We discussed at length in Section 3.1 the need for the Baseline Schedule to express customers' demand as opposed to our ability to supply. At the same time, I fully acknowledge that jobs and orders may sometimes become late by no fault of Manufacturing. Whose fault it is that the jobs become late and the reasons for which they become late are not the point. What's important is whether the jobs should either 1) continue with a heightened sense of urgency or 2) be moved to the "back of the line" with relaxed priorities.

If you choose the first option, then the Baseline Schedule should remain as-is with no change. This will ensure that the jobs remain high on the priority list in the Dispatch Lists. The second option should only come into play under special circumstances as allowed by your re-baselining policy, usually with the concurrence of the customer. You can also imagine that each of these options can affect your internal performance metrics as well as your performance as a supplier in the eyes of your customer.

Let's also acknowledge that there are some situations in which a company's schedule performance has become dire. Chances are that significant structural operating issues exist if on-time shipments remain below 80% for a sustained period of time. Repeated rescheduling is often used as a reactive coping mechanism under such circumstances. However, let's be clear: Rescheduling doesn't really solve anything. In fact, it probably just adds to operational turbulence, thus making a difficult situation even worse. Rescheduling, at this scale and frequency, is therefore tantamount to repeatedly declaring "schedule bankruptcy". Like its financial cousin, schedule bankruptcy should be regarded as a solemn process in which either a practical operating workout is pursued or the doors are closed. Hopefully this book has given you some ideas that may be useful in getting out of such a situation. My contact information appears in the front of this book for those who want additional resources to help navigate these treacherous waters.

Our objective is to maximize schedule stability so that Manufacturing can most effectively and efficiently do its job. Here are a few questions that a re-baselining policy should address in the interest of achieving this objective:

- When is it too late for a customer to request a schedule acceleration (i.e., expedited order)? How about for a schedule deceleration?

- If you do agree to accelerate a customer's order, will you require an expediting fee to offset any hidden costs (and discourage unnecessary accelerations)?

- What circumstances, if any, are non-customer (i.e., self-directed) schedule changes allowed? Be judicious with this one.

6. Enforcing Transactional Discipline

6.1. *Training Shop Floor Employees*

There are three general topic areas that shop floor operators and those that support them need to understand:

- "The Golden Rule" of transactional discipline especially as it applies to:
  - o Labor transactions
  - o Inventory transactions
  - o Non-conformance (i.e., defect) reporting
- The virtues of a pull system and its specific benefits in the areas of:
  - o Lead time
  - o WIP inventory
- Dispatch Lists: What they are and how to follow them.

We have already discussed all of these areas but I would like to suggest a practical way to show how the Dispatch Lists work and why they are able to improve the factory's performance. It will demonstrate the virtues of a pull system in the context of what the company is trying to achieve. It's called the "kanban game".

We will actually play two different versions of this game: One version will simulate a push system and the other will simulate a pull system using the Dispatch List logic. I have found that it works best with groups of 10 to 15 employees at a time in a conference room. The entire training session normally takes about 90 minutes including a short introduction about the Golden Rule, transactional do's and don'ts, the game itself, as well as a final wrap-up that explains how to follow the Dispatch Lists.

All that is needed are:

- Two sets of poker chips
- Five 8.5" x 11" sheets of paper printed with the graphics shown in Figure 24 and each numbered from one to five as shown in Figure 25. Arrange them as shown and tape them down to a tabletop.
- A single six-sided die

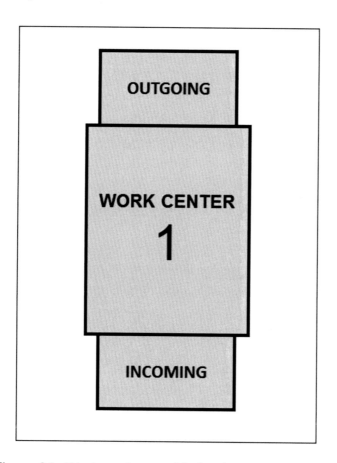

Figure 24. Work center graphic for the Kanban Game.

Figure 25. Kanban Game "factory" layout.

The game begins by placing a pile of poker chips at the beginning of the line, right in front of Work Center 1. You can use any color you like except for red. Keep only one red chip nearby and put all the others aside as we won't be using them. Each chip represents one work unit of product and the pile represents the raw material inventory. Define each work center's capacity by selecting AP and $AP(1 + N)$ values. As you recall, AP is the capacity of the production area and $AP(1 + N)$ is the maximum allowed capacity of the work center as a whole. Here are some suggested values to start out with that you should write down on each sheet of paper accordingly:

$$AP_1 = \qquad 5$$
$$AP(1 + N)_1 = \qquad 7$$

$$AP_2 = \qquad 5$$
$$AP(1 + N)_2 = \qquad 7$$

$$AP_3 = \qquad 5$$
$$AP(1 + N)_3 = \qquad 7$$

$$AP_4 = \qquad 3$$
$$AP(1 + N)_4 = \qquad 5$$

$$AP_5 = \qquad 5$$
$$AP(1 + N)_5 = \qquad 7$$

Notice that the fourth work center has less capacity than the others. This will therefore represent our bottleneck work center.

Each "day" of production involves rolling the die for each of the five work centers to see how much product is produced in each work center. The random nature of this production rate simulates the inherent variation associated with the production process. It would be useful to assign a different person to roll for each work center to increase the level of employee engagement during the game. An essential rule is to ignore rolls of the die that exceed the number of products in the production area. For example, if there are only three products in the production area and you roll a six, then ignore that roll and roll again until you roll a number between one and three.

For the push version of the game, we will only use the incoming areas. We can have an unlimited number of chips in each work center's incoming area. The "outgoing" areas will not be utilized at this time and should be kept free of chips. The maximum number of chips allowed in the production area is equal to the *AP* value defined for each work center.

Begin the first day of production by fully loading the first work center's production area by placing five chips in it from the raw material inventory. Each day of production will begin this way. The general routine you will follow for each work center is:

1. Fully load the production area using the chips in the incoming area (or in raw material inventory in the case of the first work center)

2. Roll the die to see how much product is completed

3. Move the completed product to the incoming area of the next work center.

The production line will be "dry" when initially starting the game. On the first day of production, just perform the three-step procedure just described only for the first work center. Then, on the second day, repeat the routine only for the first and second work centers. On the third day, repeat the routine only for the first, second, and third work centers. Repeat this pattern until the fifth work center produces finished product that exits the factory. We can regard the production line as being fully "wet" at this point. Make a habit of writing down the number of production days completed after managing the fifth work center. Set the day counter to zero as soon as the first finished product is produced.

Continue producing for an additional six days after the line initially becomes "wet" to ensure that the system has reached a steady state. Then, on the morning of the seventh day, introduce the red chip into Work Center 1. We will then be able to count the total number of days that the red chip spent in the factory by taking the day that the red chip exits the factory and subtracting six days of production from it thus allowing us to measure production lead time. Be sure to obey FIFO (first-in, first-out) rules so that the red chip maintains its priority position as it flows through each work center.

Write down what day the red chip exits the factory. You can continue playing at this point if you want to simulate more days of steady state production so that the production throughput metric can be more accurate.

It is time to evaluate the factory's performance after production has stopped. We will do that by calculating the three following metrics for this "push" scenario and writing the results down:

- Lead time (number of days that it took the red chip to exit the factory)

- WIP inventory (total number of chips in all five work centers)

- Production throughput (number of chips exiting the factory divided by the total number of production days)

One of the things that you may want to call attention to is the amount of work stuck in the incoming queue of the bottleneck fourth work center.

We can now begin the "pull" version of the game after we have collected all the necessary data for the "push" game. However, this time, the game will proceed using some slightly different rules necessary to effectively mimic the flow of material within a pull system. These rules embody the same logic that governs the Dispatch Lists. They are:

- No product shall be allowed in the incoming areas. Only the outgoing areas will be used.

- The quantity of product that can be moved forward is the same as what underlies our Dispatch List:

$$Q_{move} = min \begin{cases} AP(1+N) - Q_{total} \\ AP - Q_{production} \end{cases}$$

- As a consequence of our move rule, no work center can contain more than $AP(1 + N)$ total number of chips including both the production and outgoing areas added together

The game is played the same as before in all other respects including the calculation of the three performance metrics.

Table 6 shows an example of the kind of performance results you are likely to see after playing both versions of the game. Chances are that the "pull" game will demonstrate significant improvements in lead time and WIP inventory. There should, however, be little difference in production throughput experienced between the two scenarios. This is because the production rate is fundamentally limited by the production capabilities of the bottleneck work center. This is a result that is consistent with the Theory of Constraints. If there is any difference observed in production throughput between the two game versions, it is likely to be because there have not been enough days to ensure a statistically accurate result. Theoretically, if you played each scenario for a large number of days (i.e., > 200), they should converge upon essentially the same productivity results. However, we should expect some differences in observed production rates just because we are limited by playing time.

The important thing is to use this training opportunity to associate this new way of working with its benefits and the need for strict transactional discipline.

Table 6. Example of Kanban Game-end metrics.

	PUSH:	PULL:	% Improvement Using Pull
Day that red chip entered production	6	6	
Day that red chip exited production	16	14	
Total number of steady state production days	48	45	
Total number of units produced	20	20	

Lead Time (days)	10	8	20%
WIP Inventory (units)	37	14	62%
Production Throughput (units/day)	2.4	2.3	-6%

6.2. Customer Orders

The first place to monitor and enforce transactional discipline is in the entry of Customer Orders, particularly with regard to the internal due dates and customer due dates as shown in Figure 8. Standard written procedures for Customer Order entry should be developed that explain what each Customer Order date represents and how each should be managed. Setting these dates properly should ensure that adequate transit time has been planned for. Although this is a simple process, it still requires discipline on the part of the Customer Order entry specialist. Most systems set the default internal due date equal to the customer due date so that the planned transit time effectively becomes zero. This is a pitfall that should be avoided.

From time to time, some may choose to set the internal due dates for some orders extra early to "take advantage of available capacity". The problem with this approach is that the transit time then becomes variable, which has the effect of artificially distorting the Baseline Schedule and shop floor priorities. For this reason, it is better to set the planned transit times to a fixed standard time. If shipping typically takes four to five days, then conservatively set the internal due date five or six days earlier than the customer due date. Dates percolating down to the shop floor will then express customer priorities more appropriately.

6.3. Shop Floor Labor Collection and Tracking

The Golden Rule described in Section 3.3 provides the best guidance for managing shop floor labor transactions. An employee walking over to a computer and marking an operation complete, reporting his labor hours, or entering completed product quantities is the only way for the computer to really know what's physically going on.

Conveniences such as labor backflushing[2] are compelling ways to alleviate and minimize the need for manual transactions. However, you will make some sacrifices if you choose to employ backflushing. Actual labor hours and material usage may deviate from standards and the backflushed transactions may not be timely enough to enable accurate inventory levels. Why not

---

[2] *Backflushing* is a technique that can be turned on in the MRP or MES system to automatically charge materials or labor to any preceding open material or labor requirements whenever an employee inputs a manual transaction. An example of this is to automatically close and assess labor standard costs for operations 10, 20, and 30 whenever an employee manually closes operation 40.

require employees to report what they are doing directly? Is a 20-second manual transaction too much to bear? Maybe it is or maybe it isn't. These are management questions to grapple with. My position is that the best way for the computer to know what people are doing is for the people to report their actions immediately as they perform them.

6.4. Work Center Audits

For those managers who insist upon accurate manual transactions from their employees, the Work Center Audit provides an effective way to measure transactional discipline, gain insight into the practicalities of the shop floor, and train employees on best practices. The Work Center Audit focuses its attention on compliance with the Golden Rule by comparing what jobs are physically in the work center with the jobs on the Dispatch List.

The first dataset can be easily obtained in only a few minutes if the Production Orders on the floor are marked with barcodes. A portable barcode reader can then be used to quickly compile a list of all the jobs that lie within a given work center. The list is downloaded to a computer where an analysis can be performed to see where anomalies exist. Figure 26 illustrates how the data may look. The red Production Orders represent anomalies where shortfalls in transactional discipline have presumably led to mismatches between what is actually in the work center and what the system thinks is in the work center. Ideally, both datasets should match up identically with each other.

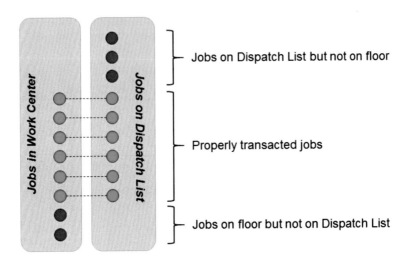

Jobs on Dispatch List but not on floor

Properly transacted jobs

Jobs on floor but not on Dispatch List

Figure 26. Work Center Audit datasets.

Setting up a database to take in the scanned Production Orders and compare them to the Dispatch List data will enable the quick generation of an audit report showing deviant Production Orders. Figure 27 shows an example of such a report. Notice that the individual that last transacted each Production Order, the date that they transacted it, and the operation that was last transacted are shown on the report. This is necessary for an effective forensic investigation and it also provides an opportunity to illuminate actual shop floor practices and provide re-training opportunities as necessary. You can also imagine creating metrics using this data to track transactional discipline by work center.

```
┌────────────────────────────────────────────────────────────────┐
│                                                                │
│                 WORK CENTER AUDIT REPORT                       │
│                                                                │
│                  Work Center: MACH03                           │
│                    4/12/2017 10:43                             │
│                                                                │
│                                                                │
│     Job ID:      Op:       Last Touched by/on/at:             │
│                                                                │
│   Found in Work Center; Not in Dispatch List                  │
│     50023       40       H. Lindt (4/10/17)    (30) MATRL01   │
│     50032       40       H. Lindt (4/10/17)    (30) MATRL01   │
│     50036       50       T. Gomez (4/9/17)     (40) CUTNGO·   │
│     50051       40       A. Macht (4/11/17)    (30) MATRL01   │
│                                                                │
│                                                                │
│   Found in Dispatch List; Not in Work Center:                 │
│     50017       45       S. Johnson (4/10/17)  (80) PAINT01   │
│     50024       40       L. Hazleton (4/9/17)  (60) CLNG01    │
│     50037       40       S. Johnson (4/8/17)   (60) CLNG01    │
│                                                                │
└────────────────────────────────────────────────────────────────┘
```

Figure 27.   Example of Work Center Audit report.

     The value of performing these audits cannot be overstated as they are essential for scrubbing inaccurate Dispatch Lists. Chief among the transactional issues you will uncover will be the phenomena of "operations left open". These are operations that were in fact completed but the required transactions were not made, thus erroneously leaving the operation open as shown in Figure 28. In this case, operation 40 will appear on the Dispatch List but the job will not physically be in the work center. Clearly, "operations left open" will wreak havoc on our MRP-supported pull system causing the Dispatch Lists to be less than reliable. Strong personnel and process management are needed to maintain a workable shop floor control system.

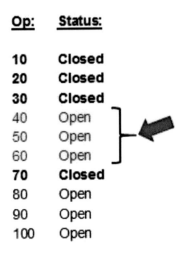

Op:	Status:
10	Closed
20	Closed
30	Closed
40	Open
50	Open
60	Open
70	Closed
80	Open
90	Open
100	Open

Figure 28. Routing example showing operations left open.

7. Putting It All Together

Whether you are searching for a transformational change or just incremental improvement in your operations, we can organize the elements of our Lean shop floor control efforts as belonging to three broad categories: Systems, practices and techniques, and culture. However, looking back at what we've covered in this book, we should realize that what we're really attempting to do is leverage our existing systems and jump-start our existing culture by introducing a series of new practices and techniques. This really is a terrific advantage since it tends not to require additional capital investment or staff. As Rumsfeld said, you go to war with the army you have, not the army you wish you had. We are therefore trying to take maximum advantage of our existing resources.

I quickly summarize some of these practices and techniques below in roughly the order that they should be implemented so that you can use it as a checklist for realizing your own *Lean MRP* shop floor control improvements:

- Customer Order date management   (Section 6.2)
- Baseline Schedule   (Section 3.1)
- Projected Schedule   (Section 3.3)
- Customer Order review and acceptance   (Section 5.1)
- Re-Baselining policies   (Section 5.2)
- Retraining employees with the "Kanban Game"   (Section 6.1)
- Dispatch Lists   (Section 4.1)
- Executional metrics   (Section 4.2)
- Work center audits   (Section 6.4)
- Archery Charts to improve schedule accuracy   (Section 3.4)

As many of you will surely nod your head to in agreement, influencing traditionally held notions and practices can often be the most difficult challenge in implementing continuous improvement. *Lean MRP* particularly falls into this category because it strikes at the heart of the shop floor operating system and therefore impacts the predominant elements of control.

This is a good place to revisit the objectives that we originally set forth, verify that they are indeed the things you seek, and contemplate how *Lean MRP* can help achieve them:

- Maximize on-time completions
- Reduce lead times
- Reduce WIP inventory
- Improve the accuracy of schedule projections

We also want to be clear about what is a production control issue, what is a manufacturing capacity issue, and what is a quality assurance issue. Scheduling, Dispatch Lists, and enhanced transactional discipline are unlikely to resolve capacity and quality problems. *Lean MRP,* however, together with strong quality initiatives and effective capacity planning can be an unbeatable combination.

Good luck and congratulations to all the operations managers bold enough to seek new solutions for overcoming practical challenges. One of the rewards of writing a book is knowing that you have helped others. Please be so kind as to keep me apprised of your successes as well as failures so that we can collectively learn through each other's efforts.

Made in the USA
Lexington, KY
27 February 2019